THE STORY OF VERONA

BY

ALETHEA WIEL

Copyright © 2013 Read Books Ltd.
This book is copyright and may not be
reproduced or copied in any way without
the express permission of the publisher in writing

British Library Cataloguing-in-Publication Data
A catalogue record for this book is available from the
British Library

Contents

The Story of Verona 1
PREFACE. 3
CHAPTER I 7
CHAPTER II 30
CHAPTER III 54
CHAPTER IV 77
CHAPTER V 115
CHAPTER VI 139
CHAPTER VII 167
CHAPTER VIII 194
CHAPTER IX 215
CHAPTER X 235
CHAPTER XI 260
CHAPTER XII 277
CHAPTER XIII 291
CHAPTER XIV 310

THE STORY OF VERONA

by

Alethea Wiel

Illustrated
by Nelly Erichsen and
Helen M. James

First Edition, July 1902
Second Edition, August 1904
Third Edition, August 1907

To
My Husband

Centrepiece by A. Mantegna, behind the High Altar of S. Zeno.

PREFACE

THE story of Verona is no simple record of a simple town with a continuous rule guiding her fortunes and directing her destinies. Her tale is mingled with that of other nations and languages; and Greek, Ostrogoth, Longobard and Frank have held sway in Verona as well as Etruscan and Roman. The influence of these diverse nationalities has left its trace on the art and history of the city to a marked extent. The architecture alone of Verona is of a nature to demand a long and deep study, and calls for an expert's hand to do justice to its different developments of variety and beauty. Her school of painting too is a subject that has not yet met with sufficient attention, and that deserves a study which hitherto has been but scantily bestowed upon it. I have tried in a humble and limited way to put before the reader some idea of this school, and to render him familiar with the names and works and methods of the masters of painting with whom he will come most in contact in his wanderings through Verona. Many of their masterpieces are to be found in the grand old churches which form one of the chief features of Verona, and within whose walls it is well to linger if we wish to grasp fully the character of the town and of the men who raised these noble buildings, and who now lie buried in or beside them. The history of Verona is all-absorbing, but I have tried to give it only that prominence which is necessary for such an understanding of the town as will interest the traveller and enable him to enjoy a stay amid surroundings that will not now perhaps seem "foreign" to him.

I have drawn much of my knowledge on the Veronese school of painting from Sir A. Henry Layard's excellent work, *Handbook of Painting. The Italian School;* based on the *Handbook of Kugler* (London: Murray, 1887), which was most kindly lent to me by Lady Layard; and to Mr Selwyn Brinton's *The Renaissance in Italian Art*, Part II. (London: Simpkin, 1898). My grateful thanks are also due to Prof. Commendatore Carlo Malagola, Head of the State Archives in Venice, for the loan of books and for help as to the means whereby to arrive at much of the information I required. I am also indebted to Cav. Giuseppe Biadego, Bibliotecario of the Biblioteca Comunale of Verona; and to Cav. Dr Riccardo Galli for help during my stay at Verona. Nor must I omit to say a word in praise of the Hôtel de Londres in that city, where comfort and economy are very happily and successfully blended by a most courteous and diligent landlord. My chief thanks though are due to Cav. Pietro Sgulmero, Vice-Bibliotecario of the Library and Vice-Inspector of the Monuments in Verona, who devoted many a spare hour to introducing me to every part of the town, and in imparting to me all he could of the knowledge he possesses in an eminent degree of the history and legends of his native town. My book owes more to him than I am able to express.

"Few towns," says Mr Selwyn Brinton, "have an individuality more delightsome than Verona—Verona the Worthy (Verona la Degna) as she was called"—and if I shall succeed in endearing that individuality and making it familiar to the traveller wandering through this "worthy" and glorious city, I shall not have laboured in vain.

Palazzo Soranzo,
Venice, *January 1902.*

THE STORY OF VERONA

CHAPTER I

Origin and Growth of the City—Verona under the Romans—Goths and Lombards in Verona—The Adige

VERONA is no exception to those great cities of Italy whose origin is wrapt in a background of uncertainty and mystery. A few scattered huts on the hillside, now known as the "*Colle di San Pietro*," were probably the beginnings of the town which was soon to spring up on both sides of the Adige—that mighty river that formed then as now such an important feature all round the country through which it flows, and whose waters have carried as great an amount of woe in their train as ever they have of weal. These faint beginnings of a mighty town bore probably some resemblance to the hamlets we now see in Umbria or Tuscany, dotted as they are on the slopes up which they seem to crawl with difficulty, and marking the sites where bastions, castles and strongholds were to stand in after times. For Verona was above all else a fortress. Her existence, as soon as she had assumed the proportions of a town, was essentially a military one, and the character stamped on her in those early days remains untouched to the present hour. It may be said of this beautiful city as of Zion of old: "Walk about Verona, and go round about her, and tell the towers thereof. Mark well her bulwarks. Set up her houses that ye may tell them that come after." This injunction to chronicle the story of the older city applies equally to the one on the banks of the Adige, and sharpens the desire to do so as faithfully and lovingly as may be.

The position of Verona, its vast military construction, its fortress guarded by three lines of separate forts, its arsenal and barracks, have made it, if not the first, at least one of the first military towns of Italy, and cause an ever-growing longing to investigate as to its origin and that of the people who founded it. That longing however has to be repressed, for all is dark and vague with regard to the early days of Verona. Her historians indeed claim for her an ancestry of fabulous antiquity: some asserting that she existed before Troy came into celebrity; others declaring that she was founded soon after the flood. Veronese writers lose themselves equally in discussions as to the race from whom sprang the inhabitants of their city and province. They devote pages to the subject and consider in turn the probability as to whether Etruscans, Rhetians, Euganeans, Celts, Cimbrians or Gauls were the founders. No satisfactory conclusion is reached. The mystery remains unsolved; and time and thought are alike wasted in

The Story of Verona

attempting to lift a veil which has been inexorably drawn by the Past, and which she defies us to remove. There can be no doubt whatever that Verona dates from very early times, even if it is beyond the knowledge of man to assert when that date exactly was. It may be assumed however that the Etruscans had a part in her foundation, and when we bear in mind that this implies a period embracing the sixth and fifth centuries B.C., the age of the city is carried back indeed to a remote epoch. The supposition most generally accepted among Veronese writers is that their town came into being about the fourth century before the Christian era, and proofs of this are forthcoming to this day in the discoveries made in and around Verona of remains of arms, utensils, vessels, tombs, and so forth, which bear witness to the different peoples who, at one time or another, were living or ruling there, and to the period of their rule. By this means, too, evidence can be found of the dominion of the Barbarians, Gauls, and Cimbrians; and indeed to remoter times still when the age of bronze, and also the neolithic age and the prehistoric age are reached in turn.

The uncertainty as to the Past clings still to the period when Rome stretched forth her conquering arms over the north of Italy. No date can be mentioned accurately as to when Verona became part of the great Republic; nor when, nor by whom the Amphitheatre, and the Theatre, which form her most classic monuments were erected. It may however be assumed that at the beginning of the third century B.C., Verona was subject to Rome. This subjection though was of a voluntary nature, and in no way arose from the right of victory. Verona was doubtless wise in time: she saw how she had everything to gain by throwing in her lot with that of Rome; and by expressing a desire to be under Roman authority and protection forestalled what would inevitably have been brought about by invasion and conquest. That this was so may be safely affirmed by the absence of all documents recording such a conquest, nor is there a chronicle which adds the name of Verona to the list of triumphs gained by any general—a triumph which would not have been omitted had it been made, nor would history have been silent over the conquest had it been there to record. It is probable that some Veronese troops came to the assistance of the Roman legions at the battle of Cannae (216 B.C.), and also that they fought for Rome against the invading forces of the Teutons and Cimbri at the close of the second century. This invasion of the Cimbri presented a danger to Rome greater than was at first imagined, and greater perhaps than any hitherto experienced by the Eternal City. The early chroniclers of Verona maintain that their city bore an important part in staving off the impending danger. They also declare that a large band of the invaders took up their abode in the neighbourhood, enchanted with the soft climate, the delicious wines (those of the Valpolicella being renowned even then), and the charms of the sunny sky of Italy. Here it is said that their descendants dwell to this day, and are still to be identified by the difference of their language, which is neither Italian nor German, though more nearly allied to the latter. The district where this diversity of language is to be found is known as the "*XIII Comuni Veronesi,*" and the "*VII Comuni Vicentini.*" Modern writers by no means endorse the Cimbrian legend, and declare that it has no foundation at all. They ascribe other causes to the philological difficulty and explain it away as follows: The proximity of Germany to this part of Italy, they contend, explains the familiarity of the Teuton tongue, together with the intercourse of the two countries and the trading that was carried on between them.

CASTEL S. PIETRO FROM THE ADIGE

The influence exercised by Rome over Verona was great; and though the chroniclers of the latter city are eager to maintain that she was in no way dependent on Rome, or unduly subjected to her, the fact remains that she was under the dominion of the Eternal City, and that Roman laws and habits were felt and adopted in the northern town. She was not admitted at once to the full rights and privileges of citizenship, though the "*lex Pompeia*" was extended to her B.C. 89, which entailed on her the rights of a Latin colony. After the battle of Philippi (B.C. 42; year of Rome 712) the privileges of Roman citizenship were granted to Transpadane Gaul; though when Verona herself was admitted to such rights cannot be affirmed with certainty. There can be however little doubt that this occurred but a short time afterwards, when she was included in the tenth region into which Cæsar Augustus partitioned Italy; a region which was known as that of "*Venetia et Histria.*" On the architrave of the Porta dei Borsari, when by order of the Emperor Gallienus the city was enclosed afresh by a wall, there was an inscription recording this fact, and proclaiming that Verona was "Colonia Augusta Nova Gallieniana." This inscription is of the more value as there is nothing beyond it to tell of the relation between Rome and Verona. No mention is made of the latter city in the records concerning the Augustan colonisations; nor is she enumerated in the list of colonies given by Pliny the Elder in his history. Tacitus speaks of her as a colony in the second century, and in the fourth century we read of Pompeius Strabo sending a colony there.

In the early days of the Roman Empire, Verona was a town of much importance; the chief cause that contributed to this importance being without doubt her geographical position. She stood at a spot where several great highways met; and all the chief roads that connected the Empire with its principal towns in the north of Italy and into Germany passed through her streets. The Gallican way (Via Gallica), coming from Brescia and leading through Vicenza to Aquileja (thus ensuring intercourse with the eastern provinces) went through Verona. So too did the Via Postumia coming from

Bedriaco. Another road led from Verona to Mantua. Another again led to Bologna. The great road to the north also started from Verona, and carried the communication from Italy into Germany, and right away to the Danubian provinces.

Ruskin[1] has described the position occupied by Verona when speaking of the view over the town as seen from the road going to Illasi. He says, "Now this promontory is one of the sides of the great gate out of Germany into Italy, through which the Goths always entered: cloven up to Innsbruck by the Inn, and down to Verona by the Adige. And by this gate not only the Gothic armies came, but after the Italian nation is formed, the current of northern life enters still into its heart through the mountain artery, as constantly and strongly as the cold waves of the Adige itself."

A great part was played by Verona at the time of the war between the Vitellians and Flavians. The latter who represented the partisans of Flavius Vespasian, and who aimed at depriving the feeble Emperor Vitellius of his crown, had taken possession of Aquileja, Vicenza, Padua, and Verona. Much fighting took place around Verona, and in the end the Vitellians were defeated, and Vespasian—whose cause had been espoused by the Veronese—became Emperor. During the third century the weakness and decay of the Empire did but gain ground. This demoralisation proceeded chiefly from internal seditions and military revolts. The host sent by Philip the Younger, surnamed "the Arab," against the Barbarians of Pannonia rebelled, and proclaimed their general Decius Emperor. Philip journeyed from Rome to quell the revolt, but when near Verona he was overcome and slain. In the meanwhile the vigour and audacity of the Barbarians did but increase. The town of Verona was looked upon as one of the keys of Upper Italy, protected as it was by the river Adige and fortified besides by walls and fortifications. Considered as a stronghold, even in the days of Augustus, its renown in that respect was but to gain ground as time went on. The Emperor Gallienus had extended the outer city walls, and in this way had rendered the town almost impregnable against the attacks of the Barbarians. This extension of the walls had been made to include the Amphitheatre, an edifice which might well be of untold advantage to a foe; for unless rescued from its outlying position it could easily be taken and turned into a formidable fort by any enemy of skill and daring. This strengthening of the walls and fortifications of Verona was accomplished none too soon. A vast federation of northern hordes, determined to take advantage of the corruption and feebleness of Rome, crossed the Alps in 268, and aimed at the conquest of Verona. They were met by the Emperor Claudius II. near the Lake of Garda, and overthrown in a great fight, when more than half their numbers were left dead on the field of battle.

In the year 312, Verona was besieged by Constantine, who bore down upon it from the pass of the Mount Cenis.

Gibbon[2] gives an account of this event as follows: "From Milan to Rome the Aemilian and Flaminian highways offered an easy march of about four hundred miles; but though Constantine was impatient to encounter the tyrant (Maxentius), he prudently directed his operations against another army of Italians, who, by their strength and position, might either oppose his progress, or, in case of a misfortune, might intercept his retreat. Ruricius Pompeianus, a general distinguished by his valour and ability, had under his command the city of Verona, and all the troops that were stationed in the province of Venetia. As soon as he was informed that Constantine was advancing towards him, he detached a large body of cavalry, which was defeated in an engagement near Brescia, and pursued by the Gallic legions as far as the gates of Verona. The necessity, the importance, and the difficulties of the siege of Verona, immediately presented themselves to the sagacious mind of Constantine. The city was accessible only by a narrow peninsula towards the west, as the other three sides were surrounded by the Adige, a rapid river, which covered the province of Venetia, from whence the besieged derived an inexhaustible supply of men and provisions. It was not without great difficulty, and after several fruitless attempts, that Constantine found means to pass the river at some distance above the city, and in a place where the torrent was less violent. He then encompassed Verona with strong lines, pushed his attacks with prudent vigour, and repelled a desperate sally of Pompeianus. That intrepid general, when he had used every means of defence that the strength of the place or that of the garrison could afford, secretly escaped from Verona, anxious not for his own but for the public safety. With indefatigable diligence he soon collected an army sufficient either to meet Constantine in the field, or to attack him if he obstinately remained within his lines. The emperor, attentive to the motions, and informed of the approach of so formidable an enemy, left a part of his legions to continue the operations of the siege, whilst, at the head of those troops on whose valour and fidelity he more particularly depended, he advanced in person to engage the general of Maxentius. The army of Gaul was drawn up in two lines, according to the practice of war; but their experienced leader, perceiving that the numbers of the Italians far exceeded his own, suddenly changed his dispositions, and, reducing the second, extended the front of this first line to a just proportion with that of the enemy. Such evolutions, which only veteran troops can execute without confusion in a moment of danger, commonly prove decisive: but as this engagement began towards the close of the day, and was contested with great obstinacy during the whole night, there was less room for the conduct of the generals than for the courage of the soldiers. The return of light displayed the victory of Constantine, and a field of carnage covered with many thousands of the vanquished

Italians. Their general, Pompeianus, was found among the slain; Verona immediately surrendered at discretion, and the garrison was made prisoners of war."

Aquileja and Modena surrendered also to the victor, and the path into Italy lay open to Constantine.

For the remaining part of that century Verona remained under the sway of the Emperors of the West, many of whom sojourned there often and willingly, attracted either by the charm of the place, or by the convenience afforded by its central position. Nor is this to be wondered at seeing how it was a very junction for Milan, Aquileja, and Germany in turn, and how it was also provided with all that was needful for the reception and accommodation of its Imperial guests.

In the following century the Veronese territory was invaded anew by Barbarians, the first inroad being that of Alaric and his Visigoths (402); the next that of the Huns under Attila. There can be little doubt that Verona fell before the armies of the "Scourge of God," but his speedy withdrawal from Italy—at the intercession it is said of St Leo—left the town again free.

The influence exercised by Rome over Verona ever since she had included her among her colonies had been felt not only in the laws and habits adopted by the northern city, but also in the religious creeds and rites practised in her midst. The worship of false gods had flourished there in early times. Eastern deities had had their services and altars, nor was the Augustan worship omitted. That this worship, which represented not only the homage rendered to the person of Cæsar but to the world-power of Rome as well, was celebrated in Verona is evident from the mention made of the "*flamen divi Augusti et Romae*" as ranking among her religious observances.

The introduction of Christianity into Verona is placed at a very early date, and one legend declares that no less a person than St Peter appointed the first bishop who was one St Euprepio. This divine, who is also said to have been one of the seventy appointed by our Lord (see St Luke, ch. x., v. i), was indeed the first bishop of Verona, but the date of his episcopate cannot be definitely affirmed, and can only be vaguely spoken of as amongst the earliest bishoprics instituted in Italy. The first bishops of Verona all attained to the rank of saints; the fourth being St Procolo, and the sixth St Lucillo, who took part in 347 at the Council of Sardis. In 380 (or according to Maffei 390) occurred the death of St Zenone, or Zeno, the eighth bishop, a man famous for his learning and saintliness of life, and who according to some traditions "reduxit Veronam ad baptismum." The writings of St Zeno have come down to the present day, and beside their doctrine and devotion have also some literary merit. It is not known where the services of the early Christians were held in Verona. The so-called grotto of San Nazzaro, of which mention will be made later on,[3] is generally looked upon as the place, and tradition has it that Divine worship was actually celebrated there. The frescoes that adorn the church are of later date than the building, and were probably added when the church was restored in the tenth century, after it had suffered much damage at the hands of the Hungarians.

That Verona possessed a bishop as early as the third century of the Christian era would point to the fact that even at that time the town contained many believers, though the martyrdoms of S. Fermo and S. Rustico in the reign of Diocletian would again demonstrate that at that epoch at all events the pagan world was in the supremacy. St Zeno's writings on the other hand assume that Christianity was widespread through the city, but this point in common with many others relating to the early days of Verona cannot be affirmed with certainty. The diocese of Verona up to the beginning of the fifth century was subject to the metropolitan jurisdiction of the See of Milan which extended (especially at the time of St Ambrose), over the greater part of the north of Italy, and was known under the Roman administration as the "vicariatus Italiae." After the death of St Ambrose and when the Imperial Government fixed its seat at Ravenna, Milan declined, its metropolitan jurisdiction was split up, and Verona with other cities in the district passed under the jurisdiction of the patriarchate of Aquileja.

The advantages that accrued to Verona from her geographical position have already been dwelt on. The disadvantages must equally be noted, chief among them being the facility with which her territory could be overrun by the wild and undaunted tribes of the North, who looked upon Italy—the garden of Europe—as the lawful reward for their labours, and who considered the trained cohorts of the Roman legions as foes worthy of their mettle.

Odoacer was the first of these invaders. He bore down upon Italy at the head of a large force of warriors, possessed himself of Rome, where he deposed Augustolo, the last Emperor of the West, and after he had imprisoned him at Ravenna, he caused himself to be proclaimed King of Italy. This was in 476, and there can be little doubt that he held sway in Verona, from whence however he was driven out in a pitched battle by Theodoric, King of the Ostrogoths. Odoacer lost heavily in the fight (489), his soldiers were carried away in the rushing, swirling waters of the Adige, when according to Eunodius "their corpses choked that grandest of rivers." Odoacer himself withdrew to Ravenna, where he was murdered in 493.

Theodoric, King of the Ostrogoths, is a name and personality associated with song and legend. His love for Verona was great, and though his official residence, so to speak, was at Ravenna, it was at the city beside the Adige that he preferred to dwell. Its strong fortifications, the convenience of its position for repelling any attack from Germany, added no doubt to the attraction felt for Verona by "Dietrich von Bern," as Theodoric was called in German ballads. Theodoric's love for Verona took shape in the several buildings which either for beauty or utility he raised in it. Baths, palaces, strongholds, and external walls were built in turn by him, and to him too is due the restoration of the aqueduct. The remains of the great palace that he built for himself on the hill of S. Pietro are still to be seen, and point to a style of architecture that had its origin in Rome. The later years of Theodoric's life are dimmed (from a Veronese point of view) by the hatred he is said to have shewn towards the Catholics. To this is ascribed among other things his destruction of the oratory of S. Stefano, at that time the Cathedral church of Verona. This deed which coincided with the German legends which easily spread to Verona confirmed the story of the demoniacal chase which was circulated about Theodoric, and which is to be found engraved among the bas-reliefs carved on the façade of S. Zeno. The legend runs as follows: Theodoric on leaving the bath mounts his horse, and followed by his hounds gives chase to a stag. The stag however always manages to escape. The hunter pursues in reckless haste and eagerness, till he finds himself brought to the gates of hell. An allegorical lesson that might have a warning not only for the king of the Ostrogoths, but for all of every class and nation who choose to heed it!

Tradition ascribes to Theodoric at one moment the building of the whole city, at other times the Amphitheatre itself, giving to this latter the name of the "House of Theodoric," just as in Rome the same name of "House of Theodoric" was once given to Hadrian's mole. Nor did legends of different sorts cease to be circulated about Theodoric in and around Verona till the fourteenth century.

The Gothic rule began to decline in the days of Totila (543), and wars in different directions around Verona, generally ending in the defeat of the Goths, proved at last their undoing. An invasion of the Greeks was however successfully withstood, though more perhaps by fortune than by skill. The Greeks had actually possessed themselves of Verona, but their greed for booty had made them careless as to securing their conquest, and before they were aware of it they were attacked by the Goths and expelled. An expedition headed by Totila's chief general Teias against the Emperor Justinian's forces under Narses was not so successful. Nor did a fresh expedition led by Totila in person fare better. The Roman and Gothic armies met at Brescello on the Po, the Goths were defeated, and Totila was slain. Teias was appointed king in his stead (560), only to die by the hand of Narses two years later, and with him the Gothic rule came to an end in Italy.

Fresh incursions from Germany again followed; but it was not till the year 568 that any permanent rule was established in Verona. That year however saw the Longobards or Lombards, under their king Alboin, pour down from the

North and spread over the fertile plain which to this day bears their name. Their rule extended to Verona, where all traces of Gothic and Grecian power disappeared before that of the new-comers.

It was at Verona that the famous banquet took place, when Alboin ordered his wife Rosamund to drink wine out of her father's skull. Alboin had conquered and killed his father-in-law, Cunimund, king of the Gepedoe, and carried about with him the trophy of his victory in the shape of the dead man's skull converted into a drinking cup. He had no settled capital in Italy, but, as Theodoric had done before him, he dwelt gladly at Verona. The story of his orgie is a well-known one, though it may be that in his drunken debauchery he was hardly conscious of the sacrilege that he called upon his wife to commit. His brutality was amply avenged. Rosamund caused her husband to be murdered (June 28, 572, or according to Maffei 574) and then fled with Elmicho (who had acted for her as Alboin's murderer) to Ravenna, taking with her Alsuinda, Alboin's daughter, and the royal treasure. The fugitives sought the protection of Longinus, the exarch of Constantinople; but soon after they reached Ravenna they were tragically put to death, and Alsuinda together with King Alboin's treasure was sent to Constantinople. According to the writings of Paul the Deacon, the Lombard historian of the eighth century, the "body of Alboin was buried by the Longobards with tears and great mourning under a staircase adjoining the palace. In our days Gilbert or Giselbert, Duke of Verona, opened the case, drew from it the sword and ornaments, and then with the vanity peculiar to the ignorant, boasted that he had seen Alboin." The whole story of the banquet, the indignity forced upon Queen Rosamund, the king's death, and all its sequel is often called in question and doubt thrown on the whole matter. The certainty of it cannot perhaps be asserted definitely, but the legend is a well-established one; and the historian Paul quoted above tells how he saw the fateful goblet, and speaks of the murder, the flight of the wife and of her accomplice, in a way which proves that he at least believed it all.

The Lombards established duchies throughout Italy, and after Alboin's death we find dukes in Verona, one of whom, Autari, married (*cir.* 589) the famous Theodolinda, daughter of Garibaldo, king or duke of the Bavarians, who exercised an important influence over the Lombard people, and who after her second marriage with Agilulf, Duke of Turin, converted them from Arianism to the Catholic faith.

In the year said to have been that of the marriage of Theodolinda and Duke Autari, the year A.D. 589, a terrible inundation of the Adige took place in Verona. The part this river played, and for the matter of that still plays, in the history of the town which it bathes and divides is marked. It rises in Lake Ressen in South Tyrol, and after a course of some 190 miles, during which it is joined by a multitude of mountain streams and torrents, it empties itself into the Adriatic. The Adige (in German the Etsch) flows down through the Brenner pass, now enclosed in narrow channels, now spreading out through lakes and wide openings, gathering force and volume, till from small beginnings it becomes the impetuous mass of waters which rushes headlong through Verona. The floods and over-flowings from this river have on several occasions wrought untold damage to the town; and but a few years ago when the spring or autumn rains had fallen in extra abundance, or when the snows were melting after an unusually hard winter, the rumour that "L'Adige ĕ in pieno" carried dread to all who heard it. This fear is almost entirely set at rest now. Great dykes and walls have been erected; the latter known as "muraglione," which are calculated to ensure perfect safety to the city, and which certainly have stood more than one test of extraordinary severity.

The inundation alluded to above is the first recorded in history; and one old chronicler asserts that so fearful a deluge had not occurred since the universal one when mankind was destroyed in the days of Noah. The country around Verona was submerged for miles, many inhabitants were drowned, and the number of corpses of beasts, as well as of human beings, floating about in the waste of waters may doubtless be held responsible for the outbreak of a grievous sickness which shortly after visited the city. The month was that of October, and the decay of autumn following close upon a long spell of heat may well have accounted for the pestilence; but the Veronese saw only the wrath of God in the calamities which befell their land and considered themselves as under a curse. This first noted inundation was not only a mark in history, it was also the occasion for a miracle—at least in the eyes of the faithful. The waters which rose to the height of several feet restrained themselves when in the neighbourhood of the church of S. Zeno. Although on a level with the windows they forbore to enter the sacred edifice, though the doors were open and would have admitted them readily had their reverential attitude not kept them outside in an upright position! There were three churches dedicated to S. Zeno in Verona, and it is impossible to say around which of the three the miracle took place. The story relating to it was told to St Gregory I. by one who came from Verona, and is spoken of by him in his Dialogues. Many investigations have been made on the subject, all alike leading to nothing and leaving the locality of the scene unestablished. In the fourteenth century the mystery was still unsolved, for Benvenuto da Imola in his Commentary on Dante was evidently in doubt over this vexed point and records as follows: "Three churches are named after San Zeno at Verona, one on the hill, another by the Adige, but this is only a small oratory or chapel, and I think it is this San Zeno of which St Gregory writes in the

Dialogues, that on one occasion the Adige had inundated Verona, but did not enter the windows of the church of San Zeno. The third church is about a javelin cast from the river, and there is no fairer church that I have seen in all Verona."[4]

The Adige, though famed chiefly for the violence of its ways and habits, has however another side to its character. Its services from a commercial point of view are great. It acts also as a highway whereby to convey heavy bales of goods, and many a raft laden with timber comes floating down its waters, which season the wood at the same time that they carry it to its destination.

A VENDOR OF FRESH WATER

THE ARENA

CHAPTER II

The Arena

BEFORE leaving too far behind us the days when Roman art and influence held sway in Verona it may be well to pause and study the monument of that past epoch which exists to this day in the shape of the Amphitheatre, and consider carefully its history in all its detail. Great uncertainty exists as to when the Arena was built. Its chroniclers, jealous to claim for it an antiquity beyond the bounds of probability, wish to ascribe it to the Etruscans; but it is Roman as to its architecture, the lettering over the arches is Roman, as is also the manner of numbering the seats of the spectators. Its age must for ever remain a mystery; the only certainty on that point being that it is very great. Some writers declare that it dates from the time of Diocletian only, and ask how is it likely that a mere Roman colony should boast a stone amphitheatre when the capital itself was lacking in such a possession? It may be answered that other towns of less importance than Verona, colonies too of Rome, were provided with arenas, some indeed grander and more elaborate than the Veronese one. It will suffice to mention those of Capua, Lucca, Pozzuoli, and Pola, to show how many existed even before the days of Augustus

Cæsar, and that there was nothing strange in Verona also having such a building long before the Colisseum came into being. It probably was erected shortly before Rome became an Empire; and it is interesting to trace the uses to which it was put as the ages rolled on their way, and brought in their train different habits and customs.

The first use for all amphitheatres was only for fights of beasts: elephants, tigers, lions, panthers, bears, even crocodiles being introduced for the purpose of warring among themselves, and proving who was the victor in the struggle for supremacy. These sports gained in extent and luxury (so-called) according to the number and variety of beasts that could be obtained; and the rarer the animal exhibited in the arena, the greater the success of the entertainment. Thus when a hippopotamus and five crocodiles appeared on the scene, the triumph was well-nigh complete! Rhinoceroses and cameleopards were introduced by Julius Cæsar, and skilled hunters on the backs of elephants were set in array to combat against them. These sports were first held in the theatres or in the circuses, but the latter were intended really for horse and chariot races; the theatres for scenic representations. The difficulties both as to seeing and performing experienced in these buildings called for another kind of edifice, and led promptly to the formation of the arenas or amphitheatres of which such beautiful specimens remain to this day showing us even in their ruined or mutilated condition on what grand and colossal lines they were erected. The theatres of Greece and Rome served to give an idea on which the needed building should be erected. A semicircle of steps, spacious and uncovered, would serve to seat the audience, then in order to accommodate more spectators and fill in the space destined for the stage, another semicircle was added, leaving a vacuum in the middle suitable for games, sports, or fights. The first amphitheatres ever built were generally of wood, a material little adapted for this kind of building, and that on more than one occasion came to grief either from fire, or from the collapse of the entire structure. The latter event occurred during the reign of Tiberius Cæsar, when at Fidena, a town of Latium, five miles from Rome, the building subsided, and 20,000 spectators according to Suetonius, 50,000 according to Tacitus, were among the number between killed and wounded.

The Arena of Verona was built of great blocks of stone, in a slightly oblong shape, 168 yards long, and 134 wide, and its arrangements for the coming in and going out of the 20,000 persons whom it could seat were admirable. The outer wall consisted originally of four stories, but of the upper one only a fragment remains, sufficient however to show how the huge curtain or veil (velarium) which covered the whole arena, and protected the spectators from the sun, was arranged and manipulated. The interior is in an excellent state of preservation; and the care lavished on this magnificent ruin ever since the fifteenth century, and continued scrupulously to this day, is beyond all praise. The plan of the building shows that it consisted of an arcade of seventy-two arches, with two tiers of boxes, and another tier with large windows. The exits (vomitori), seventy-four in number, communicated with internal staircases which led up to the steps where the spectators were seated. Nor was the question of class distinctions ignored. Seats of costly marble and highly ornamented were reserved for those of high degree; the knights were allotted places in the centre; the Roman matrons had their special quarters; the crowd was relegated to the upper part.

The first gladiatorial fights witnessed in Verona are said to have been at the beginning of Trajan's reign. These were either given as public festivals or held by private individuals; and they took place on such occasions as demanded either the celebration of a triumph, or the propitiation of the deities who watched over the dead and guided the departed spirits to the shades of the Blest. One of these latter ceremonies, judging from the letters of the younger Pliny, was celebrated in Verona during the second half of Trajan's reign. A private citizen named Maximus gave many of these sights in the Arena in honour of his dead wife, though on one occasion the entertainment failed to come off owing to a heavy storm at sea having detained the vessels which should have conveyed some panthers from Africa. Against these and other wild animals different conditions of combatants were engaged: there was a class of gladiators known as "Bestiarii," who were trained especially for the purpose; prisoners taken in war were also used; and in later times the Christians furnished many a martyr and saint, St Paul himself being of the number and telling us how he had "fought with beasts at Ephesus."

The spot where the wild animals were confined at Verona is not certain: some writers say that they were kept in subterranean cellars close to the Arena, and introduced through the gates that support the Podium.[5] Others again say, and with a greater show of reason, that they were kept in cages either of wood or iron, which were wheeled up to the Amphitheatre as they were needed. The dress of the "Bestiarii," who were also called "Hunters of the Arena," resembled that of the gladiators, and their weapons consisted only of a short dagger and a small shield. They were famed for their dexterity and their cold-bloodedness; and their address lay in avoiding the animal whom they fought, while at the same time teasing, enraging, and finally slaying him.

The Arena was also the scene of many a gladiatorial fight when men only engaged, and several mural tablets in the Museo Lapidario exist to recount the prowess of the boldest "secutore," or the most skilful "retiarius" or net thrower. One of these latter, a certain "Generoso" by name, fought no less than twenty-seven times in the Arena, while other monuments speak of the different kinds of gladiators who also performed there. The mention of their various callings shows too how every sort of combat was practised, as well as the mixed nature of the fights. These forms of sport however paled after a time, and instead of a fair trial of strength, of beast against beast, or armed men contending for the mastery, it was judged more exciting to see men, and even women and children exposed to the rage and hunger of the animals with no weapon worthy of the name in their hands and no chance of escape from a death of shame and agony. To the honour of Verona it must however be said that the number of such scenes was very limited in their midst, and that the Arena was only on rare occasions put to the purposes which so often disgraced the Colisseum at Rome.

The Arena however witnessed the martyrdoms of S. Fermo and S. Rustico, who suffered during the persecutions of Diocletian and Massimianus about the year A.D. 300. Their story is this: Fermo was a nobleman of Bergamo, and an accusation laid against him in high quarters denounced him as a Christian. A quæstor was accordingly sent to take him, and Fermo who offered no resistance was carried off with one Rustico, a humble friend who threw in his lot with him. They were brought to the Emperor, and by him consigned to the keeping of one of his councillors named Anolino. Threats, promises, tortures were employed in vain to induce them to adjure their so-called errors; and it was thereupon decided to bring them into the Arena and delight the inhabitants of Verona with an exhibition. The night before their trial the prisoners were joined by the old and saintly bishop of Verona, St Procolo, who had been wrapt in prayer with the few Christians to whom he ministered outside the town, and who now determined publicly to declare himself a Christian, ready to suffer with his brethren for Christ's sake. He came into the town, joined Fermo and Rustico, and together they were brought into the Amphitheatre. The councillor, Anolino, on beholding the old man bound, uncondemned, and a willing victim, demanded who he was, and on being told, he refused to accept St Procolo's self-sacrifice. He would not sanction a death which had not been decreed by the Emperor, and declared that the Bishop had become childish through excess of age. The poor old saint was thereupon driven out of the Arena with hootings and blows, and had no choice but to retire to his flock, lamenting that his name might not be added to those of "the noble army of martyrs." Fermo and Rustico in the meanwhile were called on to sacrifice to false gods, and their refusal to comply was followed by every kind of torture—one being that they should be roasted alive. The pile was erected, and the victims placed thereon. The flames however seized upon the executioners, and left the saints untouched, according to one legend. Another one though says that a heavy shower of rain fell at the very moment when the fire was about to be kindled, and extinguished it. This may very probably have been the case, and may too account for the power ascribed to these saints of causing rain to fall whenever it is needed. Their names are in any case invoked whenever a lengthened drought prevails, and the response generally obtained ought to convert every sceptic as to the marvellous powers possessed by these godly men. The deliverance from this form of death was declared to be miraculous; their enemies denounced them as magicians, and dragged them off to the banks of the Adige, where they were finally beheaded. This occurred on the 9th of August, and their bodies, rescued by their friends, were eventually buried under the high altar of the magnificent church which bears the name of S. Fermo Maggiore, and which is dedicated to the memory of S. Fermo and S. Rustico.

The practice of gladiatorial fights of all kinds came to an end A.D. 435; and the use of an amphitheatre seemed as though it too had reached its consummation. The invasion of the Goths and Huns brought with it a spirit of destruction as to most public buildings already in existence coupled with a need for walls, towers, and castles that was urgent and peremptory. Theodoric with all his love for Verona had no respect for this its greatest monument, and freely encouraged the removal of stones, architraves, and blocks of marble from the Arena to serve for the bastions, aqueducts, and other buildings with which he enriched the town. Nor did the

Amphitheatre fare better at the hands of Berengarius. He allowed its mighty stones to be used whenever a building, private or public, required any massive addition, and the only marvel is that it was not absolutely ruined by the wholesale plunders committed within its walls. Its use in those days was almost exclusively reserved for judicial trials, for appeals to Divine Justice, and for duels and tournaments. It also served as the place for public executions, and for the doing to death of heretics. The largest number who ever suffered for their faith was over a hundred of the sect of the "Paterani," who were brought from Sirmione in 1276, and were burned at the stake in the Arena, by order of Martino and Alberto della Scala.

Several jousts and tournaments were held here during the reigns of the Scaligers, but the only one deserving of special notice in these pages is the one given in 1382 by Antonio della Scala the illegitimate son of Cansignorio. The reason for this particular tourney was to wipe out a deed of murder, and to obliterate from the minds of the people of Verona the fact that a fratricide and a villain ruled over them. Cansignorio della Scala had laden his soul with the murders of two of his brothers in order to secure the succession to his illegitimate sons Bartolomeo and Antonio. Bartolomeo was beloved by the people, and in all ranks of society his presence was hailed with joy and affection. He was a frequent guest in the house of the Nogarola family whose palace stands not far from the church of Sant' Anastasia in the narrow street of "The Two Moors" (I due Mori). The daughter of the house, a young and beautiful maiden, aroused the love of the young lord of Verona, who had however a powerful and evidently favoured rival in the person of a noble youth of the family of Malaspina. Antonio della Scala, whose jealousy of his brother was only equalled by his ambition to reign alone, determined to turn this state of things to his own advantage, and compass his brother's death. On the evening of July 12, 1381, Bartolomeo came home from the chase weary and worn, and attended only by his secretary, one Galvani. They flung themselves to rest unconscious of the presence of some hired assassins in the room who had been concealed there by Antonio's orders. The murderers but waited till their victims were buried in sleep. They then stole quietly from their recesses and stabbed the weary hunters to death. Bartolomeo received no less than twenty-six wounds in his breast, and the murderers, favoured by the silence and darkness, proceeded to wrap the bodies in two black hooded mantles, and then dragged them to the little square of Sta. Cecilia where they threw them down close beside the Nogarola palace. The news of the murder spread like wildfire through the city, and amid clamours of horror and indignation the name of the assassin was eagerly demanded. Antonio declared that his brother had been foully done to death at the instigation of Malaspina and with the connivance of Nogarola, who had willed in this manner to avenge an outrage committed on his daughter by the murdered man. To give colour to his accusation he then proceeded to order the arrest of Malaspina and Nogarola together with the maiden, and caused them to be put to the torture so as to acknowledge their crime. Not one of the victims confessed. They preferred death to perjury; and the luckless girl succumbed to the agony of the rack sooner than declare herself guilty of a sin which she had never committed. The assertion of such innocence, even unto death, aroused the suspicions of the people, and it was not long before Antonio was denounced as his brother's murderer. The fratricide was in too secure a position to suffer the vengeance due to him, but the growing indignation and wrath throughout the city made his life far from pleasant, and he deemed it prudent to distract the thoughts of his subjects and to drown ugly facts and recollections in scenes of revelry and feasting. He was betrothed to Samaritana da Polenta, daughter of the lord of Ravenna, and he resolved to make his bride's reception in Verona the occasion for such merriment as would drive out all remembrance of the past. Troops of gaily mounted cavaliers rode out to meet the bride; others patrolled the town imparting a sense of festivity, and preparing men's mind for the welcome that all were required to extend to the fair Samaritana. Her beauty is said to have been extraordinary, and when she rode into the city in a robe of dazzling whiteness covered with gems and seated on a magnificent white steed, she was hailed with transports of delight. Courtiers, heralds, pages and trumpeters preceded and followed her, flags waved throughout the city, joyousness pervaded every heart, and the recollection of the corpses wrapped in their grim sere cloths and crying for vengeance seemed to have faded from the memory. For twenty-seven days the revels lasted; and among the jousts which took place in the Arena was one called the "Castle of Love," a joust much in vogue at that period. It consisted of an erection set up in the middle of the Amphitheatre, and representing a rock which was covered with hangings of costly velvets and silks. The loveliest maidens in Verona stood inside to defend the castle from its besiegers, armed with flowers, sweetmeats, and jets of perfumed waters. The attack was gallantly conducted and gallantly withstood! After several assaults however a host of youths from Vicenza perceived that one side of the rock was left undefended. They rushed forward, and though checked for a moment by a rain of the most exquisite comfits they stormed the breach, gained an entry into the castle and the damsels were vanquished! The rage and jealousy of the other combatants at the success of the Vicentins threatened for a moment to convert this toy war into real and deadly strife; but peace was decreed by the directors of the sports, and a grand feast given by the bride herself became the signal for universal harmony and goodwill. The cost of this banquet and of the other festivities celebrated on this occasion was enormous, and laid the taste for the expenditure and extravagance which now became the rule at the Court of the Scaligers,[6] and proved, according to one old chronicler, "the destruction of Verona."[7]

For several centuries after the fall of the Scaligers the Amphitheatre was used chiefly for tournaments and feats of arms, though for some time during the fifteenth century it was set apart as the abode of the prostitutes of the town, and stern laws were passed with regard to their inhabiting no other quarter save that alone. Under the Venetian government measures were also taken for the preservation of the Arena, and from that time forward Verona has studiously used all the means in her power to guard with scrupulous devotion this glorious memory of the Past. Some excavations made of late years have led to the discovery that water could be conveyed into it by pipes, so that nautical games and naval displays could also be given when any occasion called for such a pastime. There were also, according to Seneca, some hidden tubes laid in connection with these water-pipes, which spurted odorous water from the base of the Amphitheatre right up to the top. From there they spread like a fine drizzle through the air and were known as "the sweet-scented rains."

The last joust mentioned in history that took place in the Arena was at the beginning of the eighteenth century, when some tilting at the ring was given in honour of the

The Story of Verona

Elector of Bavaria, afterwards the Emperor Charles VII. The entertainment however failed to please the jaded tastes of that age, and it was decided to introduce bull-fighting into Verona, and degrade the Arena with exhibitions of this all unworthy order. The first bull-fight was held July 21, 1789, and met with immediate approbation. This form of sport, though new at that time in Verona, dates from a very remote epoch. It is said to have been introduced into Italy in the days when Julius Cæsar was dictator, and it was patronised later by Nero. At Verona the taste for it spread quickly, and no foreigner of note or distinction who went there failed to be present at the bull-fight which would be sure to be given in his honour in the Arena. The inscriptions which are studded about in the building, recording many of the events which have taken place there, has one which tells how the Emperor Joseph II. together with several other princes was present at a bull-fight in the month of August 1782. Another tablet records a very different scene that took place earlier in the same year when the Pope Pius VI. on his way from Vienna halted at Verona, and thousands of spectators flocked to the Arena to receive the Papal benediction. Truly the building cannot be accused of having served for nothing, nor of having reserved its walls for one kind of spectacle only! The scene must have been striking, for every corner of the vast edifice was packed, and thousands who could not find admittance overflowed into the Piazza Brà, and awaited there in solemn and respectful silence till the Pontiff raised his hands to invoke a blessing on the expectant multitude.

At the beginning of the following century the Emperor Napoleon I. sent a donation of 30,000 lire (about £1,200) towards the repairs of the Arena, and shortly after he came in person to Verona and expressed his desire to be present at a bull-fight. These fights were conducted chiefly at that time with dogs, whose training required that they should seize the bull by the ear, when the latter was considered vanquished, and the toreadores gave him the *Coup de grace*. The peril run by the hounds—generally mastiffs—was great. The utmost agility and vigilance was needed on their part to escape being gored by the horns of their adversary, and to seize his ear before he ripped up their sides. On the 16th of July 1805 Napoleon took his seat amid a vast crowd who gazed on the mighty conqueror with mixed feelings and emotions, while he doubtless felt himself to be Cæsar indeed, surrounded by the pageantry and *mise en scène* befitting his new state. A kind of shelter of a circular form was erected in the middle of the Arena wherein the assistants of the fight could take refuge if the bull became too savage. These assistants were dressed half in white and half in red, and their business was to incense the animal by waving red rags in his face, goading him with prongs and sharp sticks, and other devices tending to aggravate him beyond endurance. On the present occasion a young and vigorous bull was

The Story of Verona

turned loose into the Arena, who came on snorting, tossing the sand from beneath his feet, and showing every symptom of courage and sport. The mastiffs were let loose on to him one by one, but all in turn were overcome, and lay in the sand so many heaps of quivering, mangled flesh. At last a splendid hound, spotted black and white, was let loose, and the public admiration and expectation was centred on the graceful movements and wary gait of the dog. His mode of approach and defence was excellent, and he made more than one attempt to pin his adversary by the ear. But his skill and training were of little avail. His final leap up to the bull's ear proved fatal; the horn ripped him from end to end, and a groan of disappointment and compassion went up from the crowd as they saw the poor beast stretched on the sand in his death agony. Napoleon's interest was aroused to such an extent that he shouted out, "Loose two against him," an order promptly obeyed, but attended with no better fortune. The hounds were again gored to death, and the Emperor shouted anew, "Loose three." Again the bull was victorious. "Loose them all," cried Napoleon, and the pack was let loose. The bull surrounded by a host of foes held them at bay for a while, and with bloodshot eye and lashing tail made a gallant stand. But the numbers were more than he could contend with, and bitten, beaten and overcome, he sank upon the floor, yielding only to the inexorable doom of force. The story goes on to say that a general in Napoleon's suite, and who stood high in the Imperial favour, turned to his master and bade him draw a lesson from the scene which had just been enacted before him. He warned him to beware of any alliance that the European Powers might form against him, adding that singly he might defeat each of them in turn, but that united they might prevail against him. Another writer, describing this scene and alluding to the Emperor's presence at it, says: "A fine lesson from which he drew no profit."[8] Napoleon was present again at another bull-fight in the Arena on the 28th of November 1807. When we read that the entertainment only began at 4.30 in the afternoon, we are not surprised to learn that the Emperor left before the end, probably driven away by the gloom of evening falling ere the entertainment was half over. The last bull-fight given in Verona was in 1815, on the occasion of the Archduke John of Austria being proclaimed governor of the "Veneto." The following year the Emperor Francis I. came with his wife to Verona, but the intention of holding a bull-fight in their honour was changed to horse-racing, the reason being that the failing health of the Empress forbade of her being present at such harrowing scenes. The poor lady indeed died but a few days after in Verona on the 7th of April.

A sight of unprecedented splendour took place in Verona on the occasion of the Congress of Sovereigns that was held there in 1822. The citizens vied with each other in doing honour to the crowned heads assembled within their city walls, and among marks of revelry it was settled to illuminate the whole town, including of course the Arena. This latter part of the programme was carried out by a multitude of small lamps being ranged along the lines of the architecture, and thereby creating an impression of lightness and beauty that was almost magical in its effect. The royal guests consisted of the Emperors of Russia, and Austria, the King of the two Sicilies, the King and Queen of Sardinia, the Archduchess of Parma, the Viceroy, and the Duke of Modena. A tablet in the Arena records this Congress and the festivities held to celebrate it.

Some mention of the game of Pallone—a game peculiar to Italy, and for that reason not unlikely to prove of interest in these pages—may be made here, together with an account of how it was played in the Arena at Verona. The game itself had its origin in Greece; the Romans adopted it in their turn, introducing it into Spain and into the southern parts of Gaul, where specially walled-in spaces were built for it to be played in. At Verona it was originally played near the Ponte dei Rei Figli or Rofiolo, along the wide street known to this day as that of the Via or Caserma Pallone. The "pallone" (a huge kind of football) was over one foot and a half in diameter; it was formed of an internal bladder covered with buckskin, and inflated by means of a tool specially and very accurately made for the purpose. In modern times the players are armed with a kind of wooden bat covered with large, wooden, diamond-shaped teeth, which are so placed as to prevent the "pallone" running up the bat. The handle of this bat is hollowed in such a way as to admit of the fist passing through to grip it firmly. The players, divided in two sets, donned a costume of red and white or red and yellow. At one time all ranks took part in it, and some famous matches took place in the Arena between the champions of Verona and those of the neighbouring cities, some at times coming even from Rome.

The next use for which the Arena served was as a theatre. A small stage was set up in the grand Amphitheatre of old, and strolling companies performed there with unqualified success. Many a good cast too performed there willingly, and it was in the Arena Theatre of Verona that both Adelaide Ristori and Ernesto Rossi made in turn their début. It was then used for representations of acrobatic feats, pantomimes, gymnastics, and such like displays, finishing up with dancings on the tight rope and conjuring tricks.

All thoughts of games and frivolous entertainments were however to vanish for a while from the minds of the Veronese by the turn political events took in the year 1866, and which engrossed all Italy during the whole of that summer. Victor Emanuel II. with the aid of his ally, Napoleon III., Emperor of the French, had conquered Lombardy in 1859, and the peace of Villafranca signed after this conquest had but heightened the expectancy which then animated every patriot's breast as to the deliverance of the "Veneto." A new alliance between Victor Emanuel and the King of Prussia in 1866 had led to a declaration of war against Austria, and was quickly followed by the opening of hostilities on the banks of the Mincio. The first engagement of note was at Custozza on June 24 of that same year. The day was one of unrivalled splendour, but also of excessive heat. Since early dawn the inhabitants of Verona had flocked to the Porta Nuova, and listened with feverish anxiety as to what the issue would be of the heavy sounds which roared across the plain from the oft firing guns of the two forces. The dread and strain was not lessened when after mid-day a file of prisoners began to arrive. These were Italian soldiers taken captive by the Austrians, and they were at once lodged in the Arena, now adapted for the time being for military purposes. The grand old Amphitheatre of the Romans had served for many a baser use than that to which it was now put—a prison house for the men who had fought for their country's freedom! At eventide the wounded were brought in, and though grief over their defeat filled the heart of every citizen of Verona, the whole city was given over to the care of those who had fought so gallantly on that day. Churches and houses were all equally placed at the disposal of the wounded, and no class distinctions held back men, women and children from doing all that in them lay to succour the sufferers, be they friend or foe, victor or vanquished. The victory of Sadowa however more than obliterated the overthrow of Custozza, and the restoration of the "Veneto," and consequently of Verona, to Italy followed shortly in its train. This was in October of 1866, and in the following month Victor Emanuel came to Verona to present himself in person to his subjects as their king. The monarch's entry was greeted with cheers and acclamations, and the next day he presented himself in the Arena accompanied by his two sons, Prince Humbert and Prince Amedeus, and escorted by the Bishop of Verona, the Cardinal Marquis of Canossa; and in this historic spot the first king of a united Italy received the homage of the people of Verona. A tablet let into the wall records this visit, and, as on a previous occasion, the amphitheatre was illuminated with its myriads of little lamps.

The next occasion on which the Arena was in requisition was in 1872 when a fair was held in it for charitable purposes, and it was made to assume the appearance of an Alpine village. Forests and Swiss châlets were dotted here and there on its broad steps, booths and bright pagodas brought their note of colour into the midst of the solemn stone-work, and the locality that is said to have suggested to Dante the plan for some regions of his *Inferno* was transformed into a laughing hamlet, fitted only for merriment and brightness. In one spot were to be found light and good refreshments; in another the houses of Romeo and Juliet appeared unexpectedly on the scene; lower down the wheel of fortune offered its allurements to those who chose to make trial of its seductions; and humour, goodwill and hilarity held sway amid surroundings that certainly had never thought originally of harbouring such elements. The centre of the Arena was laid out as a garden. In the middle gurgled a fountain of wine, while round the podium a sale was carried on of the choicest wines from the Valpolicella and the Valpantena. The success of this Fancy Fair, which was held for the benefit of the Home for Children, was so great in every way that it was determined to repeat it at the end of Carnival the following year. It was accordingly done so, with the sole difference that in the centre instead of the Fountain of Wine was a most finished reproduction of the Arco de' Gavi, remodelled exactly as to size and proportions.[9]

Another weird and lovely effect obtained in the Arena was on one occasion when the citizens had all been bidden to be present at a concert given in the venerable building. Each person on arrival was presented with a small candle which they were requested to light at a given signal. The effect of these thousands of little lights starting into life as the shades of night fell, and that too from every part of the building, was very beautiful and striking, and reflected great credit on the mind which had planned so original and novel a style of illumination.

Hare and stag-hunting were also tried in the Arena, but the spot was not suited for those forms of sport, which did not besides commend themselves to the people of Verona, and they were at once abandoned. Pigeon shooting was also tried here, but that too was soon given up.

The interest aroused by aeronauts and their endeavours to travel through space had appealed in early days to the Veronese. The first efforts in such directions had been made in 1782, and the first ascent made from the Arena was nine years later. The most successful one however was in 1886, when the Marchese Pindemonte, one Signor Galletti, and the Frenchman Blondeau who directed the operations rose from within the Arena on the 6th of September and surveyed the town and country around from aerial heights. The Arena viewed from a great elevation presented, they said, the appearance of a small ribbed basin speckled with black spots, the houses beside it looked like so many dice, the belfries like small chimneys.

A new phase of gymnastic life was afterwards represented in the Arena in the shape of velocipede races, together with athletic displays, horse shows, races, and exhibitions of skill on horseback. "Buffalo Bill" also gave proof of his prowess within the Arena, and he and his Indian cowboys delighted their Veronese audience with the agility shown by themselves and by their ponies.

Thus the old walls of the Arena of Verona have looked down on scenes as varied in their nature as the ages that have witnessed them. The spirit that called such edifices into being, has certainly passed away taking with it much of the cruelty, the power, the intolerance of those days, but leaving at the same time less stamina, less endurance of soul, and less strength of character.

CHAPTER III

The Middle Ages.—Ezzelino da Romano

THE power of the Lombards, after lasting for over two centuries in Italy was now tottering to its fall, and about to give way to that of the Franks in the northern part at least of the Peninsula. The Popes seeing to their dismay that the long-bearded invaders far from confining themselves to their northern conquests were planning to add to their possessions in the South, called in the aid of the Franks. Pepin I. then King of France, answered readily to the summons; and after his death his son Charlemagne was only too glad to retain a foothold in the land where he meant to establish his dynasty. Desiderius, at that time King of the Lombards, saw clearly the danger threatening his realm. To propitiate the French monarch and bind him to his cause he gave him his daughter Desideria in marriage, little foreseeing how such a step was but to aggravate his difficulties. Desideria was repudiated shortly after her marriage, and came back to her father's house an injured, outraged woman. Desiderius swore to be revenged, though he had to conceal his intentions, and outwardly appear subservient. He sought to raise up foes against Charlemagne, who to avert the threatened sedition marched at the head of an army into Lombardy. Desiderius was defeated at Le Chiuse di Susa, and forced to fly to Pavia. At the same time his son Adelchi, whom he had associated with him on the throne, withdrew to Verona, which he fortified—a fact that proves how even at that date the town was a stronghold and able to endure a siege. It was at once beleaguered by the Franks and compelled to open its gates to them while Adelchi had to retire and seek shelter and help at Constantinople.

The changes brought about at Verona under the Carlovingian rule were many. Counts were appointed in the place of the dukes who had held sway till then; and Verona was converted from a duchy into a county, though as far as transpires the extent of territory belonging to the new condition remained unaltered. Charlemagne was in Rome in the year 781 when Pope Adrian I. baptised his two sons, Pepin and Louis, and afterwards anointed them kings. Their father's intention had been to appoint the eldest son, Pepin, King of Italy, and leave his French kingdom to Louis the second son. Pepin, as other monarchs had done before him, loved to dwell at Verona, though fate willed it, that he should die and be buried at Milan (810). The legends relating to the Carlovingian period in Verona have left a visible form in the statues of Roland and Oliver which adorn the façade of the Duomo, where the two paladins stand as though to guard the beautiful entrance to the Cathedral. Many fables are circulated as to Pepin, around whose memory a halo of love and respect has arisen which is not wholly dimmed to this day. His tomb was said to be outside the church of S. Zeno, resting between it and the church of S. Procolo; and the seat of justice where he sat and administered the affairs of state, was pointed out among the excavations on the Colle di San Pietro. There is however nothing but tradition whereon to base either of these assertions, though the people cling to them as tokens that their loved monarch lived and died in their midst.

THE FAÇADE OF THE DUOMO

The years that followed Pepin's death and wherein the Carlovingian kings extended their sway over Italy, brought no events of moment to Verona. A new line of rulers came in after the Carlovingian monarchs in the person of Berengarius I., Duke of Friuli, and his successors. This Berengarius overcame his competitor Guido, Duke of Spoleto (886) and reigned in North Italy till the year 923. The close of Berengarius's life is tragic and pathetic in the extreme. He had retired to Verona after a defeat which he had sustained at the hands of Rudolph, Duke of Burgundy. A conspiracy was here set on foot to murder him, headed by one Flambert, a noble of Verona, who stood high in King Berengarius's favour, and whose son had been held at the font by the king in person. Berengarius was apprised of the plot, and sent for Flambert to warn him in his turn. He reminded him of the love which existed between them; of the favours he had heaped on him, he pointed out to him the enormity of his crime, and the small gain that could accrue to him therefrom. At last taking a gold cup he gave it to him bidding him keep it as a pledge of the goodwill henceforward to exist between them, and reminding him that he, the king, was also his son's godfather. The same night Berengarius, to show that no trace of suspicion lurked in his mind, slept without guards, and instead of staying even within his fortified palace he caused his bed to be placed in an arbour in the garden. The next morning, as he was about to betake himself to church, Flambert, followed by some armed men, came to meet him, and making as though he would embrace him, stabbed him to death. No cause has come to light to explain the reason that prompted so foul a treachery, and the fact that Flambert was executed by the order of Milo, Count of Verona, who rushed to avenge the king, carries with it very little satisfaction.

Berengarius was succeeded in turn by Rudolph, Duke of Burgundy; then by Hugh, Duke of Provence, and his son Lothair; afterwards by Berengarius II. and his son Adalbert. These rulers were for the most part also marquises of Tuscany, and their connection with Verona did not affect her history to any great or stirring extent. Their power came to an end with Berengarius II. who was overthrown by Otho I. of Saxony, Emperor of Germany, and for a while German supremacy was paramount throughout the land. During that time a series of counts and marquises filled the office of chief magistrate in Verona. They acted, it is true, as vassals of the Emperor, but occasionally they shewed a spirit of independence and insubordination that cannot always have been reassuring to their feudal lord.

Verona was often the gathering place for Councils and Diets; and a noted one took place there in June 983, under the presidency of Otho II., when warriors, prelates, and men of letters flocked to the town from Saxony, Franconia, Suabia, Bavaria, Lorraine, and from many parts of Italy as well. The Duke of Bohemia sent his representative, nor were ladies excluded from the assembly, for not only was Otho's wife there, the beautiful Greek Theophania, daughter of the Emperor of the East, but also his mother Adelaide of Burgundy, the widow of Otho the Great. The diet was held in order to consider the ever vexed question of the sovereignty of the kingdom of Italy, and the Emperor was successful in procuring the unanimous nomination of his son Otho as future king of the Peninsula as well as of Germany.

No incident of importance disturbed the history of Verona now for some time. Her intercourse with Germany kept her trade and interests active beyond the limits of ordinary existence, without at the same time involving her in wars and dissensions over the rights and powers to be adjudged to the monarchs whether of France or of Germany, or to their rivals and foes the Popes of Rome. This state of things however came to an end when the struggle between Henry IV. and Gregory VII. blazed forth in all its violence; and men and cities were forced to take sides with either the Pope or the Emperor. Verona threw in her lot with Henry IV. Two bishops of Verona in turn subscribed to edicts published against Hildebrand, and Henry was supported anew by the town when he passed through it to wage war upon the Countess Matilda of Tuscany. Even when the Lombard cities forsook the Emperor Verona remained faithful to him, foreseeing that only in this way could religious peace be maintained, and anxious at the same time to put an end to feudalism, and to compass the introduction of the Free Communes by her own severance from the Empire.

TOWER OF THE FORMER CONVENT OF S. ZENO *The only remaining fragment of the building when the mediæval German emperors stopt on their way to Rome.*

The adhesion of the Veronese to the Imperial cause did not blind them however to their religious duties, and though no abundance of documents exists to record their prowess, there is sufficient evidence to show that the people of Verona took their share in more than one crusade, and that on two occasions their Bishops went with them.

In the meanwhile the power of the Italian Communes was working its way to the fore, establishing its principles, and binding one town after another to its cause. It failed though in laying that substratum of unity that where so many were involved could alone ensure strength; and though ignorant of its action it was gradually preparing the way for the incoming of the "signori" or tyrants who were to domineer over each town of importance throughout the Peninsula. The arrival of Frederick Barbarossa in Italy in 1154 was to test to the utmost the new power of the Communes. Verona, and many another city besides, had at first intended to stand by the Emperor, and "maintain the Imperial crown and all its honour in Italy." But such a course was rendered impossible by the Emperor's own action. His cruelty towards Milan, his ambition, his rapaciousness, convinced every inhabitant south of the Alps that they had in him an enemy of no mean order, and that every effort was praiseworthy which sought to expel him from their midst. The Veronese were eager to give evidence of their readiness to aid in so laudable an effort, and the following incident will serve to show how keen they were to hasten Frederick's departure out of Italy by fair means or foul. The story though is told only by German writers. Some native historians indeed question the narrative. They maintain that the events related never took place, and seek to exculpate their fellow-citizens from a charge of treachery over an act which, if it occurred, may be considered as that of desperate men bent on freeing their land from an invader and his forces. The Emperor Frederick Barbarossa had made one successful descent upon Italy; he had been to Rome to be crowned, and was then forced to return to Germany, his soldiers being weary of a longer absence from their homes. His way back led through Verona, "where," according to Otto von Frisingen (a contemporary chronicler and a cousin of the Emperor's), "it not being customary for the Veronese to grant a passage through their city to the Imperial arms, it was decided to build a bridge for them outside the town. On Frederick's arrival in their midst, with an army which had laid waste all Italy, the Veronese flattered themselves that the work of avenging the whole of Lombardy lay in their hands. The bridge of boats built above the city was designed for vengeance, and was a trap rather than a bridge—the boats being tied together in such guise as only just to withstand the force of the current. Huge beams of timber were in the meanwhile to be floated down the river, which beating against the bridge were to break it at the moment when the Imperialists would cross it. The plot failed through a miscalculation as to time. The Imperial troops had hastened their march so as to escape from the bands of peasants who were known to be arming against them, and crossed the bridge in safety. The timber launched for their destruction arrived only to work havoc among their foes, for it broke up the bridge, and separated a great number of Veronese who had followed on the track of the Germans from their friends; and the Imperialists falling on them put them all to the sword. The Emperor was not strong enough at that moment to avenge the intended insult; he had no choice but to continue his journey, which he did crossing the mountains into Bavaria by the way of Trent and Botzen."

This at least is the account given by the Imperial biographer; while the Veronese writers say that there is another side to the story, and that no treachery was intended. Be that as it may it certainly did not tend to improve the feeling entertained by the Emperor towards the people of Verona, while it confirmed on their side the advisability of protecting themselves as strongly as they could against the Imperial power and vengeance. For this intent they joined the League then forming in Lombardy (1164), which had for its object to arm against the common foe and fight till they had vanquished him. The League was warmly supported by Pope Alexander III., and subscribed to by the towns of Verona, Padua, Vicenza, and the cities of the Marches. This federation was soon afterwards joined by Venice, and aroused such anxiety in Frederick's mind that he hurried into Italy, collected as formidable an army as he could get together at Pavia, and determined to lay waste the country round

Verona. The allies obtained a great triumph at Vigasio, in the Veronese territory, when the Emperor without striking a blow retired from before his foes, after having stood looking them in the face for five whole days. The League gathered fresh strength from this graceless retreat. More towns threw in their lot with the Guelph faction, and Frederick's cause losing ground daily was finally overthrown on May 29, 1176, at the battle of Legnano. The peace signed after this great fight at Venice was witnessed by Bishop Ognibene of Verona, and the chief magnates of the city, among whom were the Podestă Turrisendo; Sauro di San Bonifacio, Count of Verona; two of the Avogadri family, and the Judge Cozone. The peace was signed actually at Chioggia in July, and soon after the Veronese delegates returned to their city where they were received with honours and rejoicings. Their return coincided with the completion of the basilica of S. Zeno "in pure, simple, most beautiful Romanesque style, the most perfect work of art of Veronese mediævalism."[10] An inscription tells how the works were finished in 1178, and records that in the same year in which the campanile was completed "peace was restored between the Church and the Emperor."

CHURCH OF S. ZENO. CAPITAL IN THE NAVE

Peace was however far from being the general order throughout the land. Civil and intestinal wars were rife on every side; and each town of any size or weight was split up into two factions which held either for the Pope or Emperor, or occasionally for its own cause exclusively, regardless of any interest outside the walls.

In the factions that raged between private families in Verona that of the Montecchi and Cappelletti has obtained a renown as lasting as Time itself, noticed as it is by no meaner writers than Dante and Shakespeare. The Montecchi, as head of the Ghibelline faction in the town, were also in constant strife with many other of their neighbours, especially those who belonged to the opposite faction. A contest of more than ordinary violence occurred on May 16, 1206, when the family of San Bonifacio were at the head of the Guelph party. After a fierce encounter the Montecchi were worsted and expelled from the city. Their rivals, in order to strengthen their cause, appointed Azzo VI., Marquis of Este, to be Podestà of Verona. This Azzo had formerly belonged to the Ghibelline cause, but thought it more to his advantage to change his politics and side with the Guelphs. The Montecchi though defeated were not disheartened. They allied themselves with Bonifacio d'Este, the uncle of Azzo, and his enemy from private as well as public reasons, and, their ranks swelled by Ghibelline partisans, they returned in force to reinstate themselves once more in their native city. This was in the month of August of the same year. Azzo was seated in his council chamber when his foes burst in upon him. He barely escaped with his life, and had to retire from Verona leaving all he possessed behind him. Help however came to him from Mantua and from his own followers in Verona, and he likewise returned to the charge. The struggle lasted for over a month; each tower and stronghold held by the two factions changing hands constantly during that time.

The Ghibelline faction was however the weaker one; and though they knew their cause to be hopeless they resolved to make a final and steady resistance in the only castle that yet remained to them. No hope of mercy or of pardon deceived or encouraged these desperate men. On the night of Saturday, September 8th, they awaited the on-coming of the foe, who were equally determined on their side to bring matters to an end. The attack was so well directed, the number of assailants so overwhelming, the besieged had to surrender, and were either put to the sword or taken captive. The castle was dismantled and burnt; the prisoners were sent to different dungeons; and the civil strife in the town was brought to a close for the time being. Peace however was not the normal condition of those days, and this example, cited from an old document which has come to light in recent years, is only given to show the nature and duration of these civil dissensions in a mediæval town.

The towns were not however blind to their own interests in so far as it behoved them to unite against the Emperor of Germany and prevent his gaining such a foothold in Italy as to jeopardise their liberties. The Lombard League, which had originally been formed against Frederick Barbarossa was renewed against his grandson Frederick II. in 1226 for a period of twenty-five years; and in it the cities of Lombardy swore to stand by one another, to preserve each other's rights, and to maintain mutual peace. The question of peace exercised the minds of all men in Italy at that moment absorbingly. The Pope preached it from Rome in the hopes of furthering the cause of the Crusades; the towns advocated it from motives of commerce and industry; the nobles stood in need of it for the quieting of those feuds and rivalries which were fast draining their resources and undermining the life-blood of their families. In Verona the plea for peace was advocated by a powerful Dominican preacher, Fra Giovanni of Vicenza, a member of the noble family of Schio. He met with an enthusiastic reception, for he was armed not only with the Pope's protection, but also with a purity of intention and zeal for his mission which furthered his cause immeasurably. He convoked a great assembly on the plain of Paquara, three miles outside Verona on the banks of the Adige; and on August 28, 1233, no less than 400,000 people flocked to hear him preach, and to renounce their rivalries and enmities at his bidding. "The whole population of Verona, Mantua, Brescia, Padua and Vicenza," says Sismondi, "was gathered on the plain of Paquara, and the citizens of each of these Republics collected round their magistrates and their *carroccios* (war-chariots). The inhabitants of Treviso, Venice, Ferrara, Modena, Reggio, Parma and Bologna were also there, ranged round their standards; the bishops of Verona, Brescia, Mantua, Bologna, Modena, Reggio, Treviso, Vicenza, Padua, the Patriarch of Aquileja, the Marquis of

Este, the lords of Romano, and all those of the Veneto were there too at the head of their vassals."[11]

The scene must have been a striking one, and unparalleled till then in the annals of history. Fra Giovanni ascended a pulpit in the midst of this vast concourse and harangued the crowd. He took for his text the words, "Peace I leave with you, my peace I give unto you," and commanded his audience to forgive each other their offences and to follow after peace. His injunctions were obeyed. Peace became for the moment the universal law; the factions between the families of Este and da Romano were laid aside; Guelphs consorted with Ghibellines, and foes who a few days previously had met only to stab and outrage one another now exchanged the kiss of peace and swore to remain friends.

The preacher's injunctions to forgive injuries were not observed by him himself when an excess of enthusiasm had raised him to the office of chief magistrate of Verona. He ordered the execution of sixty men and women belonging to the most respectable families of the town, whom he condemned as heretics, and who were all burnt alive.

The success obtained by Fra Giovanni at the assembly at Paquara proved his undoing. He became proud and ambitious; he aimed at becoming a ruler in those towns where he had preached peace and goodwill, and after a period of war, rebellion and imprisonment he retired to

Bologna, shorn of all glory and leaving Lombardy a prey to insurrection and strife.

Verona was no exception to this condition of affairs. Her state was torn by rival factions, the one headed by the Counts of San Bonifacio; the other by the Montecchi (or Monticoli), the latter of whom Shakespeare has immortalized for us under the name of Montague. Their faction was supported on more than one occasion by Ezzelino da Romano, who finally succeeded in making himself lord of Verona, and who was thus the first of the tyrants to oust the power of the Communes and introduce that of the "*Signori*" in their stead. Ezzelino has left perhaps the most unenviable record among all the bloodthirsty tyrants of the Middle Ages. The Florentine historian Villani says of him that "he was the cruellest and most redoubtable tyrant that ever existed among Christians. By his might and tyranny he lorded it for a long time ... over the March of Treviso, and the town of Padua, and a great part of Lombardy. He made away with a fearful part of the citizens of Padua, and blinded a great number, ever of the best and noblest among them, taking away their possessions and sending them adrift to beg through the world. And many others by divers torments and martyrdoms he put to death, and in one hour caused 11,000 Paduans to be burnt."

Nor has modern criticism passed a milder judgment on Ezzelino. Symonds speaking of him in his history of *The*

The Story of Verona

Renaissance in Italy, says: "Ezzelino, a small, pale, wiry man with terror in his face and enthusiasm for evil in his heart, lived a foe to luxury, cold to the pathos of children, dead to the enchantment of women. His one passion was the greed of power, heightened by the lust for blood. Originally a noble of the Veronese Marches, he founded his illegal authority upon the captaincy of the Imperial party delegated to him by Frederic. Verona, Vicenza, Padua, Feltre and Belluno made him their captain in the Ghibelline interest, conferring upon him judicial as well as military supremacy. How he fearfully abused his power, how a crusade was preached against him,[12] and how he died in silence like a boar at bay, rending from his wounds the dressings that his foes had placed to keep him alive are notorious matters of history.... Ezzelino made himself terrible not merely by executions and imprisonments, but also by mutilations and torments. When he captured Friola he caused the population, of all ages, sexes, and occupations, to be deprived of their eyes, noses, and legs, and to be cast forth to the mercy of the elements. On another occasion he walled up a family of princes in a castle and left them to die of famine. Wealth, eminence, and beauty attracted his displeasure no less than insubordination or disobedience. Nor was he less crafty than cruel. Sons betrayed their fathers, friends their comrades under the fallacious safeguard of his promises. A gigantic instance of his scheming was the coup-de-main by which he succeeded in entrapping 11,000 Paduan soldiers, only 200 of whom escaped the miseries of his prisons. Thus by his absolute contempt of law, his inordinate cruelty, his prolonged massacres, and his infliction of plagues upon whole peoples, Ezzelino established the ideal in Italy of a tyrant marching to his end by any means whatever."[13]

He must indeed ever rank as one of the most inhuman and brutal of monsters as far as bloodthirstiness and cruelty are concerned, but not even his bitterest foes can deny his talents as a warrior, his indomitable pluck, his energy, his presence of mind, no matter how great a difficulty encountered him, and his resource in the hour of danger. No defeat daunted him; no failure depressed him. He would originate some way out of a dilemma however inextricable it might seem; and in spite of overwhelming conditions he was never at his wits' ends for an expedient. He succeeded in making himself recognised as lord of the towns of Verona, Vicenza, Padua, Feltre, Belluno, and Trent; and no Imperial league was formed in the North of Italy which did not include him as one of its most powerful members. In May 1238 his marriage with Selvaggia, a natural daughter of the Emperor Frederick II., was celebrated at S. Zeno at Verona; and a month later on the green in front of the same church Ezzelino and the Podestà of Verona, Bonaccorso del Pal☒, swore fealty to the Emperor and to his son Conrad. Their oath was received by Pier della Vigna, the Emperor's famous chancellor, who according to Dante, "held both the keys of the heart of Frederick."[14]

Ezzelino made as short work of his foes in Verona as in other towns. Their houses were thrown down; their persons tortured and killed. The house of San Bonifacio fared badly at his hands: the castle was dismantled (1243) and stands to this day in ruins; and most of the partisans of that noble house shared grimly in the discomfiture of their chief. After a successful career of thirty-three years Ezzelino's star began to wane. His enemies—and he had many—resolved to make head against the designs he was now beginning to formulate against Milan, and opposed his forces on the Adda. He was defeated and taken to Soncino, where he died October 1, 1259, tearing open, it is said, his wounds with his own hands, preferring death rather than to see the overthrow of his schemes. The legends and fables which are circulated round Ezzelino are numerous and fantastic. Some have insisted that he was the child of the devil, no human mind and intellect being capable of committing the horrors and bloodthirsty deeds which he is said to have perpetrated. Dante places him in Hell in the "Bolgia" among the "tyrants who delighted in blood and gave themselves thereto."[15]

The death of Ezzelino da Romano marks a change in Italian politics. The power of the Communes was henceforward to disappear entirely, and that of the "*Signori*" to come to the fore. In Verona the news of Ezzelino's death, far from rousing the citizens to rejoicings over their restored liberty, awoke in them only the desire to re-establish the dignity and power of the Podestà so that in the hands of a chief magistrate their rights should be respected. Their choice fell upon Mastino della Scala, the son of one Jacopino della Scala, whose name first appears among those who formed a covenant with the people of Cremona in 1254.

THE TRIBUNA—ANCIENT SEAT OF JUDGMENT, PIAZZA D'ERBE

The Story of Verona

The mention of the Scaligers brings with it the period of Verona's greatest prosperity. The art, the literature, the romance of the city centres round the years in which the della Scalas reigned as lords of Verona, and in which they brought the town to a degree of prominence and splendour and importance which she had never reached before and to which she never attained again. The cruelties of Ezzelino da Romano were instrumental in bringing the della Scala family into notice. No less than three persons of that name had been put to death by Ezzelino, who were supposed to be some relations, even if not very near ones, of the new Podestă. The efforts made by some writers to claim an old and exalted lineage for the Scaligers has not been crowned with much success. One legend, based however on no very trustworthy foundation, says that they sprang from a man of poor, nay vile condition, of the name of Jacopo Fico, who made ladders and sold them, and that from this the family took its name. The most generally accepted idea is though that Mastino della Scala, the first of the name who sprang into notability and who may be considered as the founder of the family, was a man of modest origin, and whose line in life was of a commercial nature. His position was a prominent one during Ezzelino's reign of oppression and bloodshed; and that the tyrant had shown him some regard implies in itself that Mastino had known how to merit it. He was an absolute Ghibelline as to politics, a warrior ever ready to serve his country, and a worthy ancestor of the great men who followed him. Cipolla meanwhile bids us observe that neither as Podestà, nor as Captain was he lord of Verona in the literal sense of the words; he was only the first of the citizens, and never more than that.

OLD SEAL OF VERONA

CHAPTER IV

The Scaligers

THE rule of Mastino I. in Verona was marked by the endeavours he made to assuage the factions in the town, and to conciliate by a policy of pardon and goodwill those nobles whose politics and actions were opposed to his own. He recalled Lodovico di San Bonificio, the head of the Guelph party, and regardless of the fact that this deed excited much opposition, and provoked an attempt on his life, he followed it up by a grant of fresh pardons to Turrisendo dei Turrisendi, Pulcinella delle Carceri, and Cosimo da Lendinara, other Guelph leaders. These nobles repaid Mastino's magnanimity by organizing a rebellion to restore Guelph influence in Verona. The plot however failed; and Mastino, seeing the uselessness of showing mercy to those who had repaid him in so sorry a way, put many of the conspirators to death, and exiled the Count of San Bonificio anew.

In 1262 by the "unanimous wish" of the populace Mastino was elected "Captain of the People"; an election which proved his popularity among the lower classes of the town irrespective of that felt for him by the patricians and upper classes. Mastino was moreover successful in an expedition he organized against Trent; he also reduced

Piacenza to his rule; and gained over Cremona to the Ghibelline faction. He espoused the cause of Conradin, the last of the Hohenstauffens, and received the luckless youth at Verona in 1267 when on his way to claim the throne of Sicily. After a stay of two months Conradin left Verona, being accompanied to Pavia by Frederick of Austria and Mastino della Scala. The boy-king appointed Mastino "Podestă," or Rector of Pavia, and at the end of March 1268, he started on the fatal expedition to Sicily which cost him both his kingdom and his life.

Mastino returned to Verona to find fresh disorders and tumults in the city; and wars and fightings ensued when Bocca della Scala, one of his brothers, was killed. After much strife an important point was gained in the submission of the town of Mantua; a town that for years had headed every rise of the Guelph party, and shown the keenest animosity against Verona. This was in 1274, and Alberto della Scala, another brother of Mastino's and who was to succeed him as lord of Verona and in carrying on the dynasty, was sent at once to Mantua as "Podestă."

Three years later, on October 26, 1277, Mastino della Scala was treacherously murdered together with Antonio Nogarola who happened to be with him at the moment. No reason has been discovered for the cause of this murder. Some accounts declare that Mastino fell a victim to a conspiracy planned against him by the families of Scaramelli and

Pigozzi; others that he was striving to make peace between two inimical parties who stabbed him in return for his good offices. It has even been hinted that his brother Alberto was the real author of the assassination, but no conclusive evidence exists to countenance so foul an accusation. The scene of the murder was close to Mastino's own house, in a courtyard known as the "Volto Barbaro," not as most writers assert from the "barbarous" act here committed, but from its being the quarter inhabited by the family of the Barbaro who had their dwelling-place in that spot.[16]

Mastino's murder was fully avenged. Alberto hastened from Mantua, and passed sentence of death or of exile on those assassins who had escaped the summary justice meted out to them by the mob at the moment of the murder. Alberto was formally installed in his brother's stead, and became more powerful than his predecessor, being in fact absolute lord of Verona, and able to establish the succession firmly in his dynasty. Nor was his state confined to the limits which had bounded it in the days of Mastino. Besides confirming his rule over the Trentino, Alberto became lord of Riva, Castel d'Arco, Reggio, and Parma. Este and Vicenza voluntarily recognised him as their chief, and he also added Feltre and Belluno to his possessions. Thus an extensive territory owned the dominion of the Scaligers and the capital of this newly-formed principality was Verona. Alberto's rule was a wise one, and to some extent a peaceful one too.

There were occasional wars with many of the neighbouring towns, but none of such duration or importance as to hinder the development of art, or prevent Alberto from enlarging and beautifying the town and adding to the number of its fine edifices. "He beautified Verona with buildings," says a modern writer, "with bridges, fortified it with new walls, and in the spring of 1301 laid the first stone of the 'Casa dei Mercanti.' "[17]

Alberto was ambitious for his family, and determined to unite them by marriage with some of the princely families of Italy. His daughter Constance became the bride of Obizzo d'Este, the powerful leader of the Guelphs in Northern Italy; but the union brought more position than peace with it. Alberto allied himself soon after with Padua and Vicenza, rivals of the House of Este; and war was the consequence. The war was successful for the allies, and its conclusion was celebrated by a "curia" of a truly princely nature. A "curia" was the word in those days to signify an entertainment given to commemorate any event of moment brought to a satisfactory issue. The "curia" on this occasion was held on St Martin's day (Nov. 11), when Alberto della Scala began by conferring the honour of knighthood on some of the Nogarola, and Castelbarco family, as well as on his own sons. Bartolomeo, the eldest, was raised to this rank, as was also the youngest Francesco, afterwards so famous as Cangrande, who can then have been only about three years old. The gifts presented by the lord of Verona were not only costly but numerous, and as the condition of the donor was judged by the abundance and value of his presents, any parsimony on that head had to be avoided as certain to prove fatal to his renown. Alberto at this festival gave no less than 1500 pairs of garments, lined with fox or lamb skin, of divers colours such as scarlet, purple, deep red, green, yellow. Soon after this Alberto's eldest son, Bartolomeo, married Constance, the daughter of Conrad IV., and grand-daughter of Frederick II.

Another "curia" was held in 1298, when Alberto's second son, Alboino, was made a knight at the same time that his marriage was celebrated with Constance, the daughter of Matteo Visconti, lord of Milan. The encomiums pronounced on Alberto della Scala, who died September 3, 1301, by a contemporary Veronese historian are unbounded, and declare him to have been: "Sublime in soul, perfect in his ways, foreseeing in council, pious, merciful, sagacious";[18] and that he ardently desired all that made for the welfare of his people and of his city. In fact, according to this chronicler every virtue abounded in Alberto, who apart from his merits ranks also as the first absolute ruler of the house of the Scaligers.

He was followed by his son Bartolomeo who, according to the writer just quoted, ruled over Verona, "thinking ever of governing his people in perpetual peace." If such were indeed his object he was not always able to attain it, for several wars were waged in his reign, always though as heretofore with neighbouring towns and states. Bartolomeo della Scala may be said to have acquired more renown from literature than from history. He not only welcomed Dante to his court during the exile of the great Florentine, but his bearing towards him was ever such as to elicit from his guest expressions of praise and gratitude, tributes which the poet did not bestow readily or where he was not fully persuaded that they were deserved. In the seventeenth canto of the *Paradiso*, Dante puts into the mouth of his prophetic ancestor Cacciaguida the following lines which refer to Bartolomeo della Scala, and further on to Bartolomeo's brother Cangrande:—

> "Lo primo tuo rifugio e il primo ostello
> Sarà la cortesia del gran Lombardo,
> Che in sulla scala porta il santo uccello,
> Che in te avrà sì benigno riguardo
> Che dal fare e del chieder, tra voi due,
> Fia prima quel che tra gli altri è più tardo.
> Con lui vedrai colui che impresso fue
> Nascondo sì da questa stella forte,
> Che notabili fien l'opere sue."[19]

Nor did the literary interest attaching to Bartolomeo cease with Dante. His name is also associated with the story of Romeo and Juliet; and it is supposed that the tragedy of the two lovers, immortalised for all time by Shakespeare, took place at this epoch. There is no historical foundation for the tale of "the star-cross'd lovers," but Shakespeare has willed that it should be "in fair Verona where we lay our scene," and since a date must be determined why should it not be that which tradition has assigned to the reign of Bartolomeo?

Sufficient glory centres round Bartolomeo della Scala through Dante and Shakespeare to make the fact that he is not considered a great ruler or warrior somewhat beside the mark. He gained moreover the love of his people, of the lower classes especially, and Saraina says that when he died "it was not the great folk or the nobility who accompanied him to his grave, but the poor of the town in tears."

He was followed by his brother Alboino, a good man, but feeble, and whose anti-Ghibelline tendencies may perhaps explain Dante's contempt for him (see *Convito*, iv. 16). Commerce though flourished under Alboino, and special treaties were concluded with Venice, who saw how advantageous it would be for her to have friendly relations with a town whose position could insure such handy means of transport as those offered by the navigation adown the Adige. It is perhaps needless to add that the Queen of the Adriatic knew how to draw up the treaty in such a way as to be the chief gainer in the transaction and to secure for herself greater concessions than those granted to the Veronese.

The monotony which might have attached to Alboino's reign was relieved by his associating his brother Cangrande with him as joint ruler in Verona. This youngest son of Alberto I. was the greatest of the Scaligers, and certainly one of the greatest princes of his age. The legends that surround his life are unending and "seize on him," says Biadego, "as an infant; they follow him as a child, they environ him in his bold and lucky career as a warrior, and they accompany him to his glorious tomb."[20] The same writer tells how his mother bare him without any of the pains of child-birth, though the first sound that the new-born babe uttered reverberated through the palace. When still a child, he goes on to say, his father took him to see a great pile of gold, when the lad performed an act expressive of disdain on the heap to mark his contempt for riches. His impulsiveness in the moment of peril, his indifference to danger, and his gift of attaching his followers to him made him a keen and successful soldier; while his readiness to receive and welcome men of letters and of genius, stamp him as a prince fond of learning and of the fine arts. "The story of his conquests" (to quote again from Biadego) "is noted; his personal valour, his skill as a leader, made him in a few years lord of Feltre, of Vicenza, of Cividale, of Belluno, of Monselice, of Bassano, of Padua, and of Treviso. The rapidity of his movements, his boldness,

The Story of Verona

and above all his lust of glory were all gifts possessed by Cangrande, and celebrated by his contemporaries. Nor, say they, was he wanting in defects. He was violent with the Veronese and Vicentins in order to wring money from them; he obtained the Vicariat of Verona by purchase; nor was he free from vices. Such are the accusations brought by Ferreto of Vicenza, who, however, praises him in that he never showed himself by nature bloodthirsty. And in fact under his rule Vicenza and Padua improved; he treated his prisoner Giacomo da Carrara kindly and honourably; Albertino Mussato ... was often visited in prison by his victor, who knew how to honour his genius and the integrity of his character. Let us agree hereupon: Cangrande was a man of his times, but his great virtues redeem his small vices and place him above the princes of his day."[21]

He was also very religious; he founded the church of Sta. Maria della Scala, and together with Guglielmo del Castelbarco he gave largely to the church of S. Fermo Maggiore. His praises too were sung by Boccaccio, who pronounced him to be "one of the most noted and magnificent lords who was known in Italy since the time of Frederick II.,"[22] while the Guelph historian Villani declares him to be "the greatest tyrant and the richest and most puissant prince that has been in Lombardy since Ezzelino da Romano."[23]

The Story of Verona

At the coronation of Louis V. of Bavaria, Cangrande was present with 2,000 knights and 500 foot soldiers, all armed; and he spent more on the occasion than the Emperor and the Visconti put together. The festivals he held after the conquest of Padua lasted a month, when tournaments were held, and jugglers and minstrels were present from all parts of Europe. Cangrande was also a sportsman, and it is recorded that he kept no less than 300 hawks. Music, singers and troubadours found favour with him; a table was kept ever spread for all who flocked to it; theologians, astrologers, philosophers, met with a ready welcome from him, as did also travellers from distant lands who came probably on errands of commerce. As has been said Cangrande was a patron of learning and of the arts. Giotto came to Verona at his invitation, and though nothing remains of his labours it is known that several frescoes painted by him at one time adorned the palace of the Scaligers. The following extract taken from the *Comento Storico* of Arrivabene, gives a good and graphic account of Cangrande's court at that time:[24] "Cangrande gathered around him those distinguished personages whom unfortunate reverses had driven from their country; but he also kept in his pay buffoons and musicians, and other merry persons, who were more caressed by the courtiers than the men famous for their deeds and learning. One of the guests was Sagacio Muzzio Gazzata, the historian of Reggio, who has left us an account of the treatment which the illustrious and unfortunate exiles received. Various apartments were assigned to them in the palace, designated by various symbols; a Triumph for the warriors; Groves of the Muses for the poets; Mercury for the artists; Paradise for the preachers; and for all, inconstant Fortune. Cangrande likewise received at his court his illustrious prisoners of war: Giacomo da Carrara, Vanne Scornazano, Albertino Mussato, and many others. All had their private attendants, and a table equally well served. At times Cangrande invited some of them to his own table, particularly Dante, and Guido di Castel di Reggio, exiled from his country with the friends of liberty, and who for his simplicity was called "the simple Lombard."

The Story of Verona

THE COSTA
PALAZZO OF CANGRANDE IN THE DISTANCE
WHERE HE ENTERTAINED DANTE

Verona became in this way the home for every exile of note or of worth who sought to it, and hospitality and courtesy were, as has been seen, extended freely to all. Petrarch alludes to this when he speaks of Cangrande as "the consoler of the houseless and the afflicted," and he then goes on to dilate on what may have been some of the causes which led to the estrangement between Dante and the lord of Verona, and that brought about for a time a coldness between Cangrande and his haughty client. "When banished from his country he (Dante) resided at the court of Cangrande, where the afflicted universally found consolation and an asylum. He at first was held in much honour by Cane, but afterwards he by degrees fell out of favour, and day by day less pleased that lord. Actors and parasites of every description used to be collected together at the same banquet; one of these, most impudent in his words and in his obscene gestures, obtained much importance and favour with many. Cane, suspecting that Dante disliked this, called the man before him, and, having greatly praised him to our poet, said: 'I wonder how it is that this silly fellow should know how to please all, and that thou canst not, who art said to be so wise.' Dante answered: 'Thou wouldest not wonder if thou knewest that friendship is founded on similarity of habits and disposition.' It is also related that at his table, which was too indiscriminately hospitable, where buffoons sat down with Dante, and where jests passed which must have been repulsive to every person of refinement, but disgraceful when uttered by the superior in rank to his inferior, a boy was once concealed under the table, who, collecting the bones that were thrown there by the guests, according to the custom of those times, heaped them up at Dante's feet. When the tables were removed, the great heap appearing, Cane pretended to show great astonishment and said: 'Certainly Dante is a great devourer of meat.' To which Dante readily replied, 'My Lord, you would not have seen so many bones had I been a dog.' "

Other noble refugees who found an asylum at Verona were Uguccione della Faggiuola, lord of Pisa and Lucca, who died at Vicenza while in Cangrande's service and was honourably buried in Verona; Spinetta Malaspina, and Fazio degli Uberti.

The importance and position occupied by Cangrande in the world of letters and amongst men of note must not however make us forgetful as to the part he played as a politician. Tradition saw in him the rightful heir of Imperial ideas; and many a writer has made it clear (at least from his own point of view) that in the "Veltro" prophecy Dante intended this lord of Verona, and that it was he who was to be the "Veltro" (Greyhound) whose reign was to bring widespread good to Italy. (*Inf.* I. 101.) The controversy on that point, as is well known, has lasted for centuries, and is by no means ended yet.

Nor is this Dante's only allusion to Cangrande—assuming, that is to say, that he is indeed the "Veltro" of the first Canto of the *Inferno*. There is a fresh allusion to this lord of Verona in the thirty-third Canto of the *Purgatorio*, V. 43, which, according to Scartazzini, refers without doubt

The Story of Verona

to Cangrande. The passage is one of those mystic allusions which have puzzled the great poet's commentators in all ages, and whose enigma is yet unsolved. Dante says how that—

"Verily I see, and hence narrate it,
The stars already near to bring the time,
From every hindrance safe, and every bar,
Within which a Five-hundred, Ten, and Five,
One sent from God, shall slay the thievish woman
And that same giant who is sinning with her."[25]

"To decipher the number given by Dante," says Mr Vernon,[26] "one ought to know whether he was thinking of the symbolic value of the Latin letters, or only thinking of the letters themselves, D.X.V., which transposed, give the word D.V.X., *i.e.* a leader or captain." Whichever way one takes it, the passage evidently implies the hope that a personage would shortly appear, who would reform the Church, and re-establish the Imperial authority. It is also clear from the context that Dante is pointing to some well-known contemporary personage, on whom he could found his hopes. Scartazzini feels assured, moreover, that if this passage is compared with the prophecy of the Veltro (*Inf.* I. 100-102), it will be distinctly proved by evidence that the D.X.V. and the Veltro are one and the same person. Again, the context proves that the person foretold by Dante can only be a captain, or secular leader, and not by any means a pope or a churchman. Let us look at history. On the 16th December 1318, Cangrande della Scala, lord of Verona, was elected by the congregation of the Ghibelline Chiefs, as Captain of the League against the power of the Guelfs. It was then he actually received the standard of the Eagle, as the Leader in Italy of all the followers of the Empire. And (according to Scartazzini), it was just at the end of 1318 and at the beginning of 1319, that Dante was putting the last finishing touches to the Cantica of the *Purgatorio*. Hence Scartazzini feels quite clear that it was Cangrande della Scala who is the D.V.X. foretold by Dante. Giuseppe Picci (I luoghi più oscuri e controversi della Divina Commedia, page 158 *et seq.*), observes: "If we write down the name and qualifications of Cangrande as Kan Grande de Scala Signore de Verona," and compute numerically the initials and propositions, we have the following result:—

K	10
G	7
d	4
e	5
S	90
S	90
d	4
e	5
V	300
	515

"All things therefore concur in making it intelligible and probable that the D.V.X. is Cangrande della Scala—an opinion adopted by the majority of ancient commentators."

This is not the place to enlarge on the question, but the fact that Cangrande is considered by many Dante scholars to have been present twice over in the poet's mind as the ideal ruler of a united Empire in Italy shows how high he ranks in the opinion of thoughtful men.

There is a legend that Cangrande was among the princes present at the deathbed of Henry VII. at Buonconvento (1313), and that the dying monarch confided his empire to "lo Scaligero," "Constituens vicarium—Fidelem commissarium—Canem de Verona."

Cane tried in vain to repudiate this charge, but overcome by the pressure put on him by the other princes ... admittit—Augusti desiderium.[27]

Cangrande did not accompany Henry VII. on his progress through Italy beyond Genoa, nor was he present at his death. The legend is therefore historically impossible; "although under a mythical form," says Cipolla, "it places before us the unbiassed judgment that the Ghibellines had of the life and character of Cangrande della Scala."[28]

It was on this expedition into Italy that the Emperor conferred the office of Vicar Imperial in Verona on the Scaliger brothers, an office that owing to the death of Alboino soon after (1311) was held and exercised by Cangrande alone. On the death of Henry of Luxemburg (1313) the hopes of the Ghibellines in Italy centred round the lord of Verona; and his hopes again were set on forming a large state in the Peninsular free from suzerain lord or Emperor, and holding in his own hands the destinies of the greater part of Italy. With this object in view he asked leave of the new Emperor, Louis of Bavaria, to build a bridge over the Po at Ostiglia whereby to facilitate communication and commerce from Italy into Germany. The leave was granted, but the bridge was never built.

This scheme of Cangrande's is dwelt on by all his biographers without however arousing at the same time any accusations of ambition against the Scaliger. And this is as it should be. Cangrande's views for his country's good were of too pure and lofty a nature to be prompted by personal ambition. The greatness of soul which Dante recognised in him, and which in spite of small differences between them made the poet rank him ever as a friend, rose to visions of grandeur for his country's weal which had in them nothing sordid or self-seeking. His desire to rule over the state which in his mind's eye foreshadowed the glory of Italy was but natural, and was altogether void of any touch of self-aggrandizement. Who indeed but he could have carried out the schemes which were in his mind? Or how could another execute the designs which had originated in his brain, and that his brain alone could cope with successfully? Before however these visionary glories could take shape Cangrande died. His end came quickly and unexpectedly at Treviso on the 22nd July 1329, when he was only about thirty-eight years of age,[29] and at the very height of his glory. It is supposed that his death was brought about by an illness caused by the heat, and the fatigue consequent on his unending labours. He died, entrusting his friend and brother-in-law Bailardino Nogarola with the care and education of his two nephews Mastino and Alberto, the sons of his brother Alboino, he himself having no legitimate heirs. His body was taken to Verona, and buried in the beautiful tomb erected for him outside the church of Sta. Maria Antica, close beside the parcel of ground which forms the cemetery of the Scaliger family. Cipolla speaking of this greatest of the della Scala family says: "more fortunate than Uguccione (della Faggiuola) who lost in a moment all that he had gained, less fortunate than Matteo Visconti, who left to his valiant sons a state firmly established, Cangrande, by daily and continual wars acquired an extensive lordship, but one without stability; based only on the valour of him who formed its head. The Scaliger power disappeared rapidly in a few years after it had been founded." And again a little further on the same writer says of Cangrande: "On the field of battle brave and almost reckless as to his person, he exposed himself to every danger; he was his own general in all his warfares; though eager to rule he was faithful to his promises, and persevering in political aims. He was humane, even at times generous to the conquered; and a Paduan chronicler tells us how from having been a hard foe to the Paduans, he was as their father when he had conquered them. He coveted glory as well as dominion; and while other lords had not yet learned to hold in esteem the gifts of learning, he—not from political motives alone—received those who, through factions, had been forced to abandon their countries, and opened with splendour his palace to Dante, to Giotto, to Ferreto of Vicenza, to Sagacio Muzzio Gazzata, to Albertino Mussato. In his gilded halls he entertained with princely hospitality poets, theologians, musicians. The exile Alighieri, who had already visited Verona when Bartolomeo was lord thereof, returned under Cangrande, and although he went away thinking how

> ... *sa di sale—*
> *Lo pane altrui, e come è duro calle*
> *Lo scendere e il salir per l'altrui scale,* ...

he preserved all the same an ever grateful memory of the "magnifico e vittorioso signore di Verona," to whom he dedicated the third of his Canticles"[30] (*i.e.* the *Paradiso*).

The character of Cangrande is an extremely attractive one. His valour, his consideration for his foes, his hospitality to all who needed it, his patronage of art and learning, make him not only an admirable but a loveable figure. Nor should his labours for the good of his people and for his native town be forgotten. He revised the Statutes that Mastino I. had caused to be compiled for the government of Verona, and added another book to the five which already existed. His love of building—a love shared by well-nigh every member of his house—took shape in a fresh circuit of walls, which he caused to be erected round the city in 1324, when wars and wranglings throughout the greater part of Lombardy made the outlook threatening for Verona, and persuaded Cangrande of the advisability of protecting his city from any possible invasion. His early death must ever be deplored; and there can be no doubt that had it not been for that catastrophe many of his schemes for the greatness of Italy would have been effected, and the state of the country for one or two successive centuries materially altered. The chief stain on his memory is the share he had in the murder of Passerino Bonaccolsi, lord of Mantua (1327), from which not even his warmest panegyrists can entirely exonerate him. It can only be pleaded that considering the times in which he lived, and the habits and customs of his contemporaries, he was remarkably free from the crime—only too common in those days—of murdering every suspected foe, and that with this one exception his hands were never dyed with the blood of his neighbours.

Ruskin sums up Cangrande's doings in the following words: "He fortified Verona against the Germans; dug the great moat out of its rocks; built its wall and towers; established his court of royal and thoughtful hospitality; became the chief Ghibelline Captain in Lombardy, and the receiver of noble exiles from all other states; possessed himself by hard fighting of Vicenza also, then of Padua; then, either by strength or subtlety, of Feltre, Belluno, Bassano; and died at thirty-seven—of eating apples when he was too hot—in the year 1329."[31]

THE BACK OF CASA MAZZANTI, ONCE INHABITED BY ALBERTO DELLA SCALA

The successors of Cangrande were men of a different and entirely inferior order. Mastino, the elder of his two nephews, had certainly much of his uncle's ambition; but he had none of his greatness and loftiness of mind, still less of his talents and intellect. Alberto cared only for a life of pleasure, and was but too ready to leave the cares of office and government to his brother, provided he might follow his vicious, frivolous existence undisturbed. Verona at that moment was at the very apogee of her glory. Cangrande's victories over the neighbouring towns were bringing in rich interest as to money and position; and the Florentine historian Villani, writing of the Scaligers, says: "The rents which accrued to them from those ten towns and from their castles were more than 700,000 florins of gold, which no other Christian king possesses, unless it be the King of France. Apart from the following and the friendship of the Ghibellines, never were there tyrants in Italy possessed of such power."

The ten towns alluded to were Verona, Padua, Vicenza, Treviso, Brescia, Feltre, Belluno, Parma, Modena, and Lucca, and had Mastino but been contented with this ample heritage, his dominion would in all probability have been more firmly established. His craving to add to his state, and convert it into a united kingdom, led however to the downfall of his house. The jealousy of one or two powerful neighbours was aroused; and a sense of the danger about to spread from Verona and envelop the North of Italy became patent to all. The Florentines and the Venetians were the first to stir in the matter, and to unite against the common foe. Florence was not only afraid of an invasion of the Veronese troops, but she also wished to regain possession of Lucca, which had been wrested from her at a very inopportune moment. The Venetians had a grievance, and that a serious one, though of a different nature, against Mastino. He had built a salt factory between Padua and Chioggia, where every Venetian vessel as it passed along the Brenta was called on to pay a tax. The Venetians were not disposed to accept quietly an affront offered them on territory which they considered as strictly their own, and they at once put in a claim for redress. No notice being taken of this appeal, Venice gladly threw in her lot with Florence, and the league between the two Republics was soon after joined by the houses of Este, Visconti, and Gonzago. The league was further strengthened in a strange and unexpected way by Marsilio da Carrara's desire to unite himself with the other allies against the lord of Verona. This son of the former lords of Padua was keen to expel the Scaligers from his native town, where Alberto della Scala had been appointed governor by his brother Mastino. Alberto, as has been said, lived only for pleasure. He had outraged the wife of Ubertino da Carrara, Marsilio's cousin, but, far from imagining that such an insult could rankle in the husband's mind, he placed blind confidence in him and in Marsilio, never dreaming that they were determined to avenge the outrage which he for one had so completely forgotten. Marsilio was well aware of the enmity felt towards the della Scalas at Venice, and determined to turn it to his own account. Chance also favoured him. Mastino sent him on an errand to Venice, where the legend goes that one night at supper sitting next to the Doge, Francesco Dandolo, Mastino whispered to him, "I wish to speak to you." Upon this the Doge dropped his napkin, and both men bent down to pick it up. "What will you give to him who gives Padua to you?" asked Marsilio. "The lordship thereof," was the reply; and when the two heads reappeared above the board the bargain was struck, and the league which was to end in Mastino's overthrow was formed.

Marsilio returned to Padua, and set to work at once to put his schemes into execution. Mastino's fears were aroused, and hints of what was brewing found their way to his ears. Again and again he wrote to Alberto warning him against the Carraresi, and bidding him be on his guard. Alberto gave no heed; and Mastino finally wrote a letter ordering him to arrest them and arrange for their execution. This letter arrived with instructions that it was to be given into no hands save Alberto's; but he, absorbed at the moment in a game of chess, handed it to Marsilio, and bade him read it. Marsilio did so, and in answer to Alberto's queries as to its contents, replied that it was only a request from Mastino to send him some more falcons. He then left the room, sent directions to the allied force under the ill-fated and peerless Pietro de' Rossi to march upon Padua when he would admit them through one of the gates into the city. These directions were all successfully carried out. Padua was lost to the Scaligers; Alberto was sent as a prisoner to

Venice, and Mastino's power received a shock from which it never recovered. He had presently to cede Belluno to Charles, King of Bohemia, who had also joined the league against him; and shortly afterwards that monarch possessed himself of Feltre, Cividale, and the Cadere as well. Brescia and Bergamo surrendered to the Visconti; and in December 1338 Mastino was glad to make peace with the allies and content himself with a state reduced to the four towns of Verona, Vicenza, Parma, and Lucca. It was not long however before the two latter cities were also wrested from him.

These concessions and humiliations exasperated Mastino past all bearing. He became suspicious and irascible, a prey to doubts and fears, and in August of that same year in a fit of ungovernable fury he transfixed Bishop Bartolomeo della Scala with his own sword. This murder brought down on him the thunders of the Church. He was excommunicated by Pope Benedict XI., and it was not till after much negotiation and the payment of a fine that the ban was removed. There is a legend in Verona that after the murder of the Bishop and the Papal excommunication Mastino II. never shewed his face again even to his faithful and beloved wife Taddea da Carrara. This legend may arise from the fact that the equestrian statue over his tomb is represented with the visor drawn—a proof, it is said, of the desire he had to veil himself from every eye, and to prevent everyone, even after death, from gazing on his features.

Before Mastino's death two brilliant marriages took place in his family; the first being that of his daughter Caterina with Barnabŏ Visconti, the heir to the duchy of Milan. The bride's name, originally Caterina, was changed to Beatrice, to denote her worth and merits; and then on account of her queenly bearing it was turned again to Regina.[32] The other marriage was that of Cangrande II., Mastino's eldest son, with Elizabeth, daughter of Louis of Bavaria. Mastino lived but a short time after these marriages. He died in 1351, leaving three legitimate sons: Cangrande II., Cansignorio, and Paolo Alboino. His brother Alberto did not survive him long. He gave over the cares of office absolutely to his three nephews, and died in the month of September of the following year.

TOMB OF MASTINO II. DELLA SCALA

Cangrande II. who now succeeded to the chief power was neither a great nor a good man. He was nicknamed "Canis rabidus," though who gave him the name, or why it was given, has not come to light. He loaded his people with taxes, and made his rule so unpopular that a rebellion raised against him by his natural brother, Fregnano, met with ready support from Cangrande's subjects and almost proved his undoing. Cangrande had gone from Verona to Botzen to confer with his brother-in-law the Margrave of Brandenburg, leaving the town in the charge of Fregnano and Azzone di Correggio. Fregnano roused the citizens to revolt; the Gonzagos of Mantua—to whom every rebuff given to the Scaligers meant a gain to them—joined the rebels; and it is generally supposed that Barnabŏ Visconti, lord of Milan, was not as opposed to the rising as in his capacity of a loyal brother-in-law he ought to have been. Fregnano, according to Giovanni Villani, was "beloved by the people of Verona and Vicenza," and his cause was warmly espoused by the great mass of the populace. Cangrande however retraced his steps as soon as he heard of the rebellion; he entered Verona with haste, and at once attacked and defeated Fregnano, who fell fighting at the head of his troops on the Ponte delle Navi.

The danger was averted, but Cangrande's confidence in his so-called allies of Milan and Mantua was destroyed for ever. His plans for insuring his personal safety at all events against any further peril took shape in the erection of the "Old Castle," the Castel Vecchio, which he now caused to be built beside the Adige, adding to it that fine bridge which spans the river, and across which he could receive aid from Germany whenever he required it. The building took three years to complete, and when it was finished Cangrande removed into it and passed the rest of his life there. He also introduced a special bodyguard of soldiers from Brandenburg, who have left traces of their sojourn in Verona in the shape of the little church of St Peter Martyr, said to have been founded by these Knights of Brandenburg.

Cangrande II., who was neither loved nor respected by his people, died a violent death on December 14, 1339, being put to death by his brother Cansignorio, who slew him with his own hand. Cangrande left three sons: Tebaldo, Guglielmo, and Fregnano, none of whom reigned as lords of Verona, and of whom history has no stirring deeds to relate.

Cansignorio was proclaimed lord of Verona and Vicenza together with his younger brother Paolo Alboino. The latter however was never admitted to any share in the government; and after a few years Cansignorio, fearing the young man's ever-increasing popularity in Verona, caused him to be imprisoned. Opinions as to the character of Cansignorio are not invariably unanimous. Some writers, among them our own Ruskin, have been carried away by a fictitious glamour concerning this last legitimate ruler of the Scaligers which facts and history cannot altogether support. Others see in him only a fratricide, stained whenever it suited his purpose with the blood of his brothers, with no redeeming virtues save that of an interested solicitude for the welfare of his people and for his native town. As usual in such judgments, there is doubtless a good deal of truth on both sides, though few, perhaps, can be found to agree altogether with Ruskin, who speaks of him as "a prince who had in every way beautified and cared for the city; and among other minor gifts, bestowed on it one by which it profits to this day, the fountain of the great Square. He was deeply religious; meditated constantly on his death, and believed that he should be entirely happy in the next world if only he were assured of the prosperity and secure reign of his children in this one."[33]

PONTE SCALIGERI. BRIDGE OF CASTEL VECCHIO

Cansignorio, in common with all the princes of his house, had an insatiable love of building, and many an edifice in Verona bears witness to his taste and munificence in this respect. The greatest proof of it is to be seen in the magnificent tomb which he caused to be erected for himself during his lifetime, and of which mention will in time be made. He also embellished and improved the town in every possible way, spending with a lavish hand, and with a recklessness which almost savoured of extravagance. He rebuilt the Ponte delle Navi; he laid out the public gardens near his palace; he added to the frescoes in his own house; and the many statues and adornments that he caused to be set up in Verona gained for the town the surname of "Marmorina." The greatest public benefit he ever conferred was that mentioned by Ruskin of bringing drinkable water into the city. This he did by means of leaden pipes laid down to the Piazza delle Erbe, where the beautiful fountain in the middle stands as a record to this day of the good deed wrought for the city by Cansignorio della Scala. He also did all that lay in his power to alleviate the sufferings of his people, when from the years 1369 to 1371 they were stricken with famine; and in many ways he shewed himself a wise and considerate ruler.

His love for his two natural sons however blinded him as to all sense of right and wrong; and his eagerness to secure the succession for them after his death made him absolutely unscrupulous, and a murderer. These sons, Bartolomeo and Antonio, were Cansignorio's only children, but their illegitimacy barred their right to reign after their father, and made Paolo Alboino, Cansignorio's youngest brother, the rightful heir. Cansignorio however was determined that his sons, and they only, should be lords of Verona when he died. Though still a young man—he was not yet thirty-six—he knew that his end was approaching, and he laid his plans accordingly. A few years previously, as has been said, he had imprisoned Paolo Alboino at Peschiera. The unfortunate youth, who was much beloved by the people, was now put to death at the instigation of his brother, it is generally supposed, though some writers lay the murder at the door of Cansignorio's sons. The most honourable and exalted of the citizens were then called on to take the oath of allegiance to Bartolomeo and Antonio; the youths were entrusted to the care of Cansignorio's most faithful councillors and friends; and on October 19, 1375, this last great lord of Verona died.

The Story of Verona

FOUNTAIN IN THE PIAZZA DELLE ERBE
(Statue said originally to be of the 3rd century)

Bartolomeo and Antonio reigned for a few years conjointly. Bartolomeo, the elder, and who was generally acknowledged as the best of the two, was treacherously murdered July 12, 1381, and his brother was declared to be the murderer.[34] As sole ruler of Verona Antonio strove to protect himself from the perils which were fast gathering up against him from the lords of Milan and of Padua. He entered into an alliance with Venice, little foreseeing that the great maritime republic had no idea of protecting him, but dreamt only of increasing those possessions on the mainland which it was now her ambition to add to her dominions. The doom of the Scaligers was sealed. Antonio had alienated the two friends, Guglielmo Bevilacqua and Giacomo del Verme, whose wisdom and prowess in the council-chamber or on the battle-field could yet have upheld his power. His extravagance, joined to that of his wife, Samaritana da Polenta, was hastening to exhaust a failing exchequer; the power of the Visconti, and of the Carraresi was every day assuming proportions of a threatening and overwhelming nature; and help was nowhere to be looked for nor obtained. Antonio endeavoured to restore his fallen fortunes by resorting to arms, and more than one important engagement took place between his forces and those of Padua under the famous English condottiere John Hawkwood, and Giovanni d'Azzo. The Veronese troops were commanded first by Cortesia Serego, and after the first defeat when he was taken prisoner, Guglielmo degli Ordelaffi and Ostasia da Polenta were appointed as generals. They met with no better fate: the armies of Verona were again routed, and Antonio without a friend to stand by him or advise him, stole secretly away from Verona the night of the 18th November 1387, handing his town over to the ambassador of Wenceslaus, king of the Romans. Verona was apportioned to the duchy of Milan, and the day after Antonio's flight the banner of the Visconti waved over the town. Antonio fled to Venice, but he did not give up all hope of returning to Verona and resuming his sway there. The following year he opened negotiations with Carlo Visconti, a son of Barnabò's, and he also essayed to gain the Pope Urban VI. over to his cause. He died though before any of these dealings could be concluded (August 1388) leaving his wife and family in such straits that they had no choice but to accept the bounty that the Venetian Republic vouchsafed to bestow upon them. Antonio left one only son, Can Francesco, who died in 1392, only four years after his father, and in him the male line of the Scaligers came to an end.

Several years later an effort was made to restore the rule of the della Scalas in the person of Guglielmo, one of the illegitimate sons of Cangrande II. The plot however failed; Guglielmo died a few days after he had been proclaimed lord of Verona, and the hopes of restoring the dynasty of the Scaligers were at an end for ever. Their rule had lasted for one hundred and twenty-eight years, and it certainly comprised the brightest, most stirring period in the annals of the town of Verona.

OLD SHIELD OF THE SCALIGERS

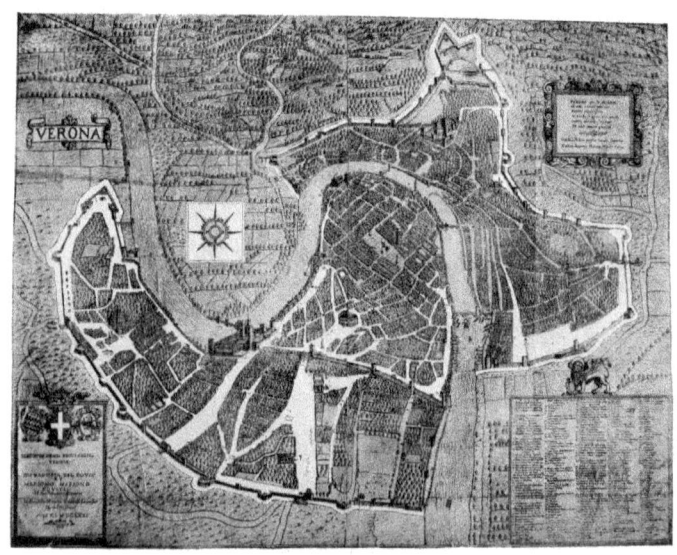

CHAPTER V

From the Fall of the Scaligers to the Present Day

THE head of the house of Visconti at the moment when Verona was added to the duchy of Milan was Gian Galeazzo, one of the most treacherous and ambitious tyrants of his age. In the league formed between him, the Republic of Venice, and the Carraresi of Padua, it had been arranged that Verona should be ceded to the Visconti, and Vicenza to Padua. This compact was now carried out, though Gian Galeazzo by guile and force soon after wrested Vicenza from its destined owner. At Verona the princely system of building carried on so grandly by the Scaligers was still maintained. The fortifications already existing round the town were renewed; the castles of S. Pietro and S. Felice (this latter sometimes known as Castelnuovo) were erected by order of the lord of Milan, who doubtless hoped in this way to ingratiate himself with the Veronese besides providing for his own safety. Gian Galeazzo did not however win the love of his new subjects, who, though they had hated Antonio della Scala, hated still more the man who had stepped into his rights and usurped all the power of the Scaligers. The lord of Padua, as was natural, had also little cause to love the Visconti, who had failed in keeping his engagements towards him and tricked him out of his right to possess Vicenza. A plot was organised to reinstate Can Francesco, Antonio della Scala's only son in his father's rights; and da Carrara and his son lent their services on the understanding that in case of success Vicenza should be restored to them. The plot failed however and Ugolotto Biancardo, who governed Verona in the Visconti's name, ordered the town to be given over to fire and the sword, and for three whole days a hideous pillage went on.

Can Francesco died in 1394, and no further revolts for the restoration of the Scaliger dynasty disturbed the rest of Gian Galeazzo's reign. His life however was not a long one, he died aged only fifty-five years on September 3, 1402, leaving his sons too young to administer his vast and scattered states and appointing his widow, Catherine Visconti (who was also his cousin), regent of the duchy.

The confusion that ensued on the duke's death spread throughout the greater part of Italy, and raised the hopes of those lords who had been dispossessed by him of their states to regain their own again. Each one in turn thought the moment had come for this purpose, and that no time should be lost in bringing about so laudable an object. The Carraresi thought it advisable for them to further the cause of the della Scalas, and help them to regain the lordship of Verona, seeing that in such an act many advantages would accrue to them. Francesco di Carrara consequently persuaded Nicolò III. of

Este to unite with him in advancing the claims of Guglielmo the illegitimate son of Cangrande II., on Verona, and for a short while success attended their schemes. The attention of the Visconti party was exclusively absorbed by affairs in Lombardy; the allies were free to march upon Verona, where the inhabitants greeted Guglielmo with enthusiasm, and shouts of "Scala, Scala," echoing throughout the town proved what a hold the once loved dynasty still had on the hearts of the citizens. Guglielmo was however a dying man when he entered Verona; weariness and disease had almost done their work on his exhausted frame, excitement and emotion doubtless did the rest. He died the very day after his joyful entry into the home of his ancestors, leaving two sons, Brunoro and Antonio, who for a few days remained in Verona under the delusion that they would succeed to the honours which had seemed to be within their father's very grasp. Guglielmo's death has been laid at Francesco da Carrara's door, but there is no evidence to prove this accusation, though the fact that the Carraresi seized on the persons of Guglielmo's sons and carried them off prisoners, does not altogether help to lighten the charge. Francesco da Carrara was then proclaimed lord of Verona, though his enmity with Venice ought to have made him wary as to the acquisition of power and territory which he knew were coveted by her. The great Republic, ever since she had become possessed of Treviso, had watched with a jealous eye any increase of dominion on the part of her neighbours. In an ill-advised moment for herself, she coveted property on the mainland, forgetful that her strength and wealth sprang from the sea, and in that quarter only should she have concentrated all her energies. The proclamation of the Carraresi as lords of Verona filled the Venetians with envy, and determined them to secure so fair a possession for themselves. They despatched an army under Jacopo del Verme into the Veronese territory, but the first engagements were won by the troops of Jacopo da Carrara, Francesco's son. This was early in 1405, and in the spring the fighting began again. The Veronese however were tired of this condition of things: they were not anxious to own the house of Carrara as their lords; and they willingly consented to place themselves under the Venetian rule. Verona accordingly passed under the dominion of Venice, and the act testifying to this surrender was signed, June 22, 1405.

The Venetian yoke cannot be said to have pressed heavily on Verona. Her independence, it is true, no longer existed, but the blessing of peace was hers; the conditions as to the forms of government were honourably maintained, and though Venice studied the preservation of the city for her own advantage more than for that of the inhabitants, this self-interest did not fail to benefit all concerned. The Republic of St Mark busied itself with the completion of the walls and fortresses which the Visconti had begun; and also made good the damage done to those buildings in the past days of insurrection and pillage.

A slight demonstration in favour of the Scaligers took place early in the fifteenth century when Brunoro, the son of Guglielmo della Scala, prevailed on the Emperor Sigismund (with whom he was a great favourite) to plead for him with Venice, and obtain some at least of his ancestral rights in Verona. The Venetian Republic refused however to listen to this appeal, and Brunoro aware of the hopelessness of his cause dedicated himself entirely to the service of the Emperor, and died at Vienna, November 21, 1434, without leaving any lawful issue.

The wars waged by Venice against Filippo Maria Visconti, Duke of Milan, brought reflected suffering upon Verona; and the honour—as far as it went—of receiving such famous generals as Francesco Sforza, and Gattamelata was poor compensation for the sums of money the town had to give the "condottieri" of the Republic in order that they might keep their troops from pillaging the city.

The effects of the League of Cambray were also fraught with momentous issues for Verona. This league, formed with the object of compassing the overthrow of Venice, was supported by most of the crowned heads of Europe. The jealousy aroused by the "insatiable cupidity," the ambition, and the prosperity of Venice was felt principally by the King of France, the Emperor of Germany, and the Pope.

In the distribution that these potentates had made of the Venetian territories on the mainland Verona was allotted to Germany; and Maximilian I., who was then Emperor, had already formed visions of an extended empire into Italy, of which he had settled that Verona was to be the capital. The condition of Venice was indeed critical. The combination of forces destined to crush her was colossal, and she was in need of all her statecraft and ingenuity to avert a catastrophe that seemed bound to overwhelm her. She took a desperate resolution which has in turn been ascribed to the subtlest heights of diplomacy, and to the very depths of despair and terror. She released all her subjects on the mainland from their oath of allegiance, setting them free to meet the emergency of the moment in the way they judged most expedient, and absolving them from any after reproach of infidelity should they elect to bow to the on-coming storm. Up till now Verona had always stood loyally by Venice in her warfares and struggles with other states, but the present danger was of a kind involving risks which she would not and could not run. The upper classes had not become enamoured of Venetian rule, and the remembrance of the Scaligers had left its hold fondly in their hearts. The populace on the other hand were wholly Venetian in their thoughts and affections, but they were not strong enough to maintain their opinions unaided, and had to succumb to the inevitable. Their attitude however to the Venetian forces, when after their defeat at

Ghiarraddada they presented themselves discomfited and weary outside the gates of Verona was hardly that of subjects who had lived for years under a just and liberal rule. A modern writer,[35] himself a Veronese and an ardent patriot, admits that not only should they have allowed the armies of their countrymen to find shelter within the walls, but they should gladly and courageously have shared with them in the discomforts and chances of a siege. The population, as we have seen, was divided: one part holding for the Venetians, the other for the Imperial cause. To this latter faction known as that of the Marani, from the name of their leader and captain, the famous painter Falconetto belonged. He himself lived in the neighbourhood of S. Zeno, and he persuaded a large number of the inhabitants of that district to side with him. One reason of this strong feeling for the Imperialist cause is to be found in the traditions of Veronese history. Verona was essentially a Ghibelline city; her brightest era was associated with Ghibelline rulers; she was the metropolis in Italy of the Emperors of Germany, the capital of their vicars, and when the days of her splendour were over, then, and then only, had she become a provincial town of the Republic of Venice. Her sympathies were for the Empire as opposed to the Republic, and at a solemn meeting convened on May 30, 1509, in the church of St Anastasia—when the entire population was present—the Emperor Maximilian was unanimously accepted as sovereign lord of Verona.

The Venetian governors and commandants withdrew quietly and without uttering one word of protest, and in October of the same year the Bishop of Trent (George of Neudeck) entered the town in his capacity of Imperial lieutenant. The Emperor himself arrived in Verona a day or two after, in full pomp and state, under a panoply of cloth of gold, his raiment being of the same costly material and his appearance, according to the Venetian chronicler, Sanudo, being that of a "Cæsar of the days of old."

He at once issued a Proclamation, which is a quaint bit of reading, now full of loving words and phrases, now reminding his new subjects of the vileness of their former masters, and insidiously hinting that they had better remember their duty and allegiance to the Cæsar of to-day. This Imperial decree also congratulates the Veronese on their good fortune in having escaped from "the intolerable servitude and the cruel tyranny of the Venetians." It holds out the happiness that is in store for them, the first they will enjoy under the shadow of the Just and Puissant Lord who they now obey. They are not to be deluded nor deceived, but must persevere in the faith and devotion and observance towards this Liege Lord. If they will but confide absolutely in him they shall be embraced with that benignity, favour, and grace with which that same Lord embraces all his faithful subjects ever ready as he is to succour them, to load them with increase, honour, and comfort. To prove still more his goodwill to the town, the Emperor restored the mint which had fallen into disuse since the days of the Carraresi, and went so far as to cause some coins to be struck with the proud motto, "Verona Civitas Metropolis." How these flattering and caressing promises were to be kept Time soon showed! The town was reduced to the state of a vast and disorderly barrack. German, French, Spanish, Italian soldiers, without discipline, without pay, rampaged through the streets bent only on booty, and reckless as to their way of securing it. Many a house and shop, the abode till then of quiet citizens and honest burghers, was ruthlessly sacked and ruined, and many a one who, rightly or wrongly, was suspected of favouring the Venetian party, was wantonly murdered in the streets without more ado. Money was also exacted on all sides in order to furnish the vast sums needed for the expenses of the war, and, as the writer above quoted justly remarks, the luckless city was indeed the "civitas metropolis" of every public and private misfortune. The internal divisions became daily more accentuated under this condition of things. The aristocracy upheld the authority of the Emperor in the hope that by so doing they would augment their own; the lower classes in the meanwhile sighed for the quiet they had enjoyed under the Venetian Republic. Nor were these divisions and tumults the only trials that overtook Verona at that time, for a terrible pestilence fell on the city in the years 1511 and 1512, filling up the cup of woe that seemed already full to overflowing. Another burden was however about to be added to those that had gone before. In 1516 the Venetians besieged the town, assisted by the French, who but a few years previously had been their deadliest foes, but were now their allies and friends. The treaty of Brussels at the close of the year fortunately put an end to the siege, and Verona was soon after restored to Venice. A series of forms had to be gone through before the transfer was effected. Verona was handed over first to Spain, then passed on to the French general Lautrec, who received it in the name of his master Francis I., and from him again it was restored to Venice. The act of restitution was accompanied by a great religious function in the Cathedral: high mass was celebrated, and a general pardon was proclaimed on the part of the Signory of Venice to all at Verona. It is strange to read how that here and there some stone lions of St Mark, which had been stowed away during Maximilian's reign in Verona, were now brought out from their hiding-places covered with decorations, and set up with every sign of rejoicing. Peals of bells rang out cheerily, cries of "Marco, Marco," re-echoed through the streets, fireworks and illuminations lit up the darkness of the winter night, and the French invaders could not contain their surprise over the kindly feeling entertained by the people of Verona for Venice. To mark still further the satisfaction felt by the people over the restoration of the Venetian rule, the beautiful column that stands at the northern end of the Piazza delle Erbe was erected in 1523. It is a magnificent block of white Veronese marble, and the year following the winged lion was placed on the top, that emblem of the wavering Evangelist whom the great Republic took for its Patron and its Saint.

THE PIAZZA DELLE ERBE, WITH THE VENETIAN COLUMN

That wary Republic, fully alive to the dangers through which she had passed, was resolved to provide against any which might assail her in the future. The fortifications around Verona were consequently ordered to be put into a condition to meet the modern requirements of war; old fortresses were to be demolished, and new ones put in their stead with bastions, moats, and all the contrivances then considered requisite to render the town impregnable. The old walls were only retained on the side towards the hills, where assaults were considered unlikely, or at the most harmless. It was while these works were in construction that new entrances into the town were voted necessary, and the following were therefore erected, namely—the Porta Nuova (1541-42), that of the Palio (1542-57), Porta Vescovo (1520), Porta S. Zeno (1541-42), and the far less well-built one of S. Giorgio (1525). These works were done by Michele San Micheli, a native of Verona, and one of the greatest architects Italy ever produced. His fame chiefly rests on all buildings connected with military matters, though in other edifices, whether of a religious or a lay nature, his work ranks very high.

An insurrection was set on foot in 1522 to stir up the Veronese against the dominion of Venice, and to restore, in the person of a pretender, the line of the Scaligers. The wars between Francis I. of France and Charles V. of Spain had let loose a great number of restless, turbulent spirits, whose aim was to attain to some position of eminence and honour by the upsetting of the existing forms of government. One of these intriguers, a Spaniard it is supposed, gave himself out as Bartolomeo della Scala, and managed so far as to secure a promise of provisional support from Spain, and from the House of Gonzaga. The Venetian Republic was fully aware of the intrigue. She just waited for the moment when it suited her best to strike, and then she did so effectively. She accepted the offer of a hired assassin to remove the pretender from her path, and when he was soon after poignarded in the streets of Mantua (1529), she clenched matters by condemning the dead man's son, Brunoro, to be imprisoned for life in the fortress of Famagosta.

For over two centuries no movement of political importance stirred the even tenor of life at Verona. A terrible plague in 1630 swept away more than half the population, and reduced the number of inhabitants, it is said, from over 50,000 to barely 20,000. Another misfortune overtook the town in 1757, when the Adige overflowed its banks (September 2), swept away two arches of the Ponte delle Navi, and wrought untold damage.

Greater and graver disturbances were, however, in store for Verona at the close of the eighteenth century. It was then that, after a sojourn of twenty months, Louis XVIII., under the assumed name of Count de Lille, left the town owing to the political intrigues gathering on all sides, and threatening to involve every state which harboured him.

Bonaparte's victories were now bringing that great general every day nearer to the Veronese district; and after his victory over the Austrians at Borghetto di Valeggio he feigned great indignation against Verona for harbouring the royal fugitive. He announced his intention to possess himself of the town, and the Venetian Republic, now too weak to claim an authority it was unable to exercise, had quietly to acquiesce in Bonaparte's occupation of Verona on June 1, 1796.

The following digression as to the Comte de Lille's sojourn in Verona, taken from a "Raccolta ... di Documenti[36] Mediti" belonging to the diplomatic story of the Revolution and Fall of the Venetian Republic may prove of interest here. The Comte de Provence (to give him his real name) had fixed his abode in Verona towards the end of the year 1794, under the incognito of "Comte de Lille." His mode of life was quiet and private, and though his suite recognised him as Louis XVIII., King of France, he himself avoided every outward semblance of majesty so as not to compromise the Venetian Republic, which had afforded him an asylum and hospitality in its territory. The nobles of Verona took no heed of him; and even the French emigrants in the city abstained from paying their court to him, keeping themselves prudently in the background. The Count was lodged in the palace of the patrician family of the Gazzola, and while there, with the help of his most trusted followers, he set to work to prepare some despatches, which he intended eventually to send to the sovereigns of Europe, in order to ascertain their measures with regard to him. In the meantime he meant to remain quietly at Verona, and there to await the tide of events. Several persons of note came expressly to Verona to greet him, among them being the Count d'Entragues, the Prince of Nassau, and the Spanish Ambassador, the Chevalier de Las Casas. That he had received every courtesy from Venice is evident by a letter that he wrote to Alvise Mocenigo the Venetian envoy, on the expiration of that nobleman's term of office in Verona, to thank him for the civilities that had been extended to him, and begging him likewise to convey his gratitude to the Doge. This letter bears date June 18, 1795. The Comte de Lille however wrote other letters, which were not altogether of so simple an order. The very next month it was discovered that he had despatched two letters to the King of Sardinia, the first of these being to announce his succession to the throne of France, and written as though he were actually a king; the other in a confidential strain, implored the King of Sardinia to continue his hospitality to the writer's wife, Marie Josephine of Savoy, Countess of Provence. The King of Sardinia took notice only of the second of these letters, though explaining at the same time that he could take no line of action about it till he knew what would be the conduct of the Allied Courts, especially those of Vienna and London. The Countess of Provence was allowed to stay on at the Royal palace, where but a few Frenchmen went to pay their homage to their so-called queen.

Early in August of this same year a slight Royalist movement was known to be on foot, and the suspicions of M. Lallement, the French Plenipotentiary from Paris in Verona, began to be aroused. The Venetian Government shared the uneasiness clearly shown by the Frenchman at the state of affairs, the more so, as they were strangely, not to say nervously anxious, to maintain scrupulously the terms of armed neutrality on which they stood with regard to other nations. Their uneasiness was in no way lessened at M. Lallement's objection to the residence in Verona of His Royal Highness the Count of Provence, whom the French journalists styled derisively "the King of Verona." In the meantime the French army was preparing to invade Italy, a measure that was frustrated for a short while by the opposition offered to such a step by the joint action of the Piedmontese and Austrian forces. The Venetian Government all this time remained passive, making no preparation to meet the on-coming danger, and careful only not to infringe the neutrality to which they considered themselves exclusively bound. This attitude of theirs, and their apathy as to the suspected plots on behalf of the Comte de Lille at Verona, provoked the indignation of the French powers in Paris. A ministerial note was addressed to Alvise Querini, the Venetian ambassador in the French capital, to remonstrate. It dwelt on the harmony to be desired and maintained between the two Republics, a harmony however that could not tolerate "so crying a scandal as that of the residence in Verona of Louis Stanislaus Saverio, the so-called Louis XVIII., who proclaimed himself, and acted as King of France." It further stated that "since Louis Stanislaus Saverio had not feared to compromise the Venetian Republic in behaving while in Venetian territory as King of France, he had forfeited all claim to the asylum which he had obtained ... and the Minister of Public Affairs asked that he should be deprived thereof throughout all the states of the Venetian territory." A string of complaints followed this verbose note, together with a remark couched in a truly ironical spirit, as to the improbability of the French Republic allowing so indiscreet a guest to be tolerated any longer, and the sad dilemma in which the Venetian Government must doubtless find itself. The agitation subsequent on the publication of this despatch in Venice was great. The "Savii," urged by M. Lallement to send a prompt answer, invoked the assistance of the Inquisitors of State, and they again despatched their secretary Giuseppe Gradenigo to Verona, while the Count d'Entragues sent a special messenger to inform the Comte de Lille of the turn things were taking. The Marchese Carlotti was deputed to present himself to the Royal exile, and break to him that the Venetian Government could not but carry out the injunctions laid on them by the French rulers. The luckless Count could offer no opposition to this law of the strongest, but he made an effort to maintain the dignity of the House of Bourbon, and claimed the right to erase his family's name from the "Libro d'Oro" of Venice, and to take back the suit of armour presented of old by Henry IV. to the Republic. He wrote to the Russian ambassador in Venice, complaining of the treatment he had received at the hands of the Venetians, and entrusting him with a power of attorney to execute his commission as to the Libro d'Oro and the suit of armour. His letter ran as follows:—"Louis, by the Grace of God, King of France and of Navarre to Monsieur Mordino, Privy Councillor to H.M. the Emperor of all the Russias, and his Minister Plenipotentiary to the Republic of Venice, Chevalier of the Order of Vladimir, greeting.

"The Senate of Venice having notified in an offensive manner that the asylum which We had elected to choose ceased from this instant, and that they expected Us to leave Verona in the shortest possible time, We have replied in these terms to the Marquis Carlotti, charged to deliver this commission directly to Us:—I shall depart, but I exact two indispensable conditions:—1st, that the Libro d'Oro, where the name of my family is inscribed, be brought to me, that I may with my own hand erase it therefrom; 2nd, that the suit of armour be restored to me which was given by my ancestor Henry IV. as a token of friendship to the Republic of Venice. The lawful impatience which We have to withdraw from the

Venetian states determines Us to empower you on Our part to execute the fulfilment of these two conditions, to cancel the name of Our family from the Libro d'Oro, and to receive in custody the suit of armour of our ancestor Henry IV. of glorious memory.

"L.S. Given at Verona under Our sign and ordinary seal the 20th April, year of grace 1796, and of Our reign the first.—Louis."

These conditions of the would-be King of France could not however be complied with. The reply to his demand was only arrived at after a long correspondence had been carried on between the Venetian Republic and the Court of St Petersburg, and was altogether unfavourable to the Count's wishes. The name of the Bourbons, it said, could not be erased from the Libro d'Oro without causing dire offence to the sovereigns of Spain, Naples, and Parma, all of whom belonged to the family of the Bourbons, nor for the same reason could the armour presented by Henry IV. to Venice, and jealously guarded by her, be now given back. Thus Venice gained her point on all sides. The Count of Lille was banished from the territory of the Republic, and on the 15th April 1796, at three o'clock in the afternoon, he wended his way from Verona to seek in the direction of the Tyrol for the shelter and safety that were no longer to be afforded him beside the banks of the Adige, and where for twenty months he had enjoyed a calm, if not a real home.

Nor did Venice forego her possession of the princely gift bestowed on her by Henry of Navarre. That suit of armour is to be seen to this day at the arsenal at Venice, though the sword which belonged to it was stolen in 1797, and not the least clue exists as to where it is now to be found. To return however to Verona.

The occupation of the town by the French was of short duration, for the Austrian troops under General Wurmser swept down on the valley of the Adige the very next month, and entered the town the 30th of July. Their stay however was also brief. The French returned as conquerors on August 8, and the victories of Arcole and Rivole confirmed them in their possession. They were not beloved by the people of Verona, of whom the greater part considered themselves still subject to Venice, and resented the military occupation foisted on them by Napoleon. What brought matters to a climax is unknown, but on the evening of April 17, the first shot was fired, and the Veronese rose up in arms against the French. A very wholesale massacre ensued, though the assertion that the inhabitants of Verona spared none of their foes, and even fired on the hospitals, slaughtering both sick and wounded in their fury, is probably an exaggeration. Fighting, firing, cannonading, the ringing of bells to call to arms went on for three whole days. French troops came hurrying in to the defence of the French, who poured a ceaseless rain of bullets on to the town from the forts, till

The Story of Verona

the Veronese had no choice but to surrender. The Venetian authorities commenced the negotiations for ceding the town, and on April 27 the French again took possession of Verona without—and to their honour be it said—this time insulting the vanquished or abusing of their victory. The "Pâques Véronaises," the Veronese Vespers, as this rising and massacre has been styled, may be considered in a twofold light. It may either be looked upon as the only effort made to uphold the dying power of Venice; or it may be reckoned as a useless waste of blood and treasure. It certainly did not tend to conciliate the French towards the inhabitants of Verona; and it gave Bonaparte an excuse for avenging the blood of his soldiers—an excuse he was not the man to forget. Heavy taxes were laid on the city; citizens of renown and high degree were executed; and wherever tyranny and oppression were possible they were indulged in freely.

The French yoke became so obnoxious that when in 1798 the town was handed over to the Austrians it seemed to the Veronese as though a stroke of good fortune had befallen them. The Austrian possession this time lasted till the peace of Luneville, early in 1800, when the city was divided between the French and Austrians, the French retaining the half on the right bank of the Adige, the Austrians reserving that on the left bank. This condition of affairs lasted till 1805, when the whole town was declared to be French, and when Napoleon caused himself to be proclaimed king of

Italy, appointing Eugène de Beauharnais as his viceroy. In 1814 Verona again changed hands, being placed once more under the Austrian dominion, after Napoleon was fallen from his high estate, and when the might and determination of England had stopped him from enslaving and oppressing the greater part of Europe.

For many years Verona belonged to Austria. The Lombard-Veneto kingdom, ruled over by the Archduke Rainer, brought outward peace to the country from which it took its name, though the longing to expel the foreigner and create a united and independent kingdom of Italy was growing and developing in the heart of every true patriot throughout the Peninsula. This longing took shape in 1848, when the war of independence was begun. The hopes of freedom and unification centred round Charles Albert and the small kingdom of Piedmont, and at the outset fortune smiled on the gallant undertaking. The Austrians however were not to be driven lightly out of the country; they reconquered Milan; possessed themselves anew of the "Veneto"; and inflicted a severe defeat on the Piedmontese army at Novara (March 23, 1849). No sooner were they firmly established again in Verona than they set to work to restore the fortifications and build new ones all around and about the town. They converted it into a fortress of the very first rank, and made certain that from the great quadrilateral—formed of Verona, Mantua, Legnano, and

The Story of Verona

Peschiera—they had a base of operations which would render them impregnable against any attack. And indeed it seemed as though Austrian rule was fixed for all time in the North of Italy. Plots and intrigues, it is true, were constantly being formed, but they collapsed without accomplishing their aim, and were never sufficiently serious to unsettle the ruling powers.

It was not till the year 1859 that the patriotic hopes which had dawned more than eleven years previously began again to see the light, though the perfect day was not to be reached even then. Napoleon III., Emperor of the French, did all that in him lay at that period to help his ally Victor Emanuel II. to the possession of his entire realm. The peace of Villafranca, however, put to flight the hopes that Solferino and S. Martino had formed, and though a part of the Veronese territory was restored to Italy, the town itself and much of the province remained subject to Austria. This state of things lasted till 1866, when the Prussians became the allies of Italy, and the Austrians were finally driven out of the Peninsula. The great battle of Sadowa, resulting in the peace of Vienna (October 3, 1866), settled definitely the vexed question as to the rights of ownership, and on the 16th of the same month the Italian army entered Verona in triumph. Far different must have been the feelings with which the Austrians quitted it. True, the town did not stand on their native soil, nor was the language spoken therein their mother tongue. But years of possession had endeared it to them; they had guarded it with unceasing love and care; they had made it one of the finest fortresses of Europe. Now all was to be changed. They must hand it over to the young and newly-formed kingdom of Italy, and who could assure them that all would be well with the town in other and inexperienced hands? Time alone was to furnish the answer.

On November 18th, 1866, King Victor Emanuel II. and his sons Humbert and Amedeus of Savoy came to Verona. The day following they were present at a great concourse of people held in the amphitheatre. An enthusiastic welcome awaited them; the national joy burst spontaneously from thousands of spectators, proving the affection of the Veronese for their rightful princes, and convincing the king and his children of the love and loyalty that existed for them in the grand old city of Verona la Degna.

CHAPTER VI

Men of Letters—School of Painting

A LOVE of letters and a regard for men of learning has ever been a marked characteristic throughout the history of Verona, and stamped the early and after days of her existence with a special and distinctive note.

The first name on a long and honoured roll is that of Valerius Catullus, who was born at Verona about B.C. 84. As all classical students know he owned a villa at Sirmione, where the ruins of an old mansion are pointed out as the abode of the "tenderest of Roman poets nineteen hundred years ago"—the poet who might well be called the Heine of his age.

The province of Verona claims Cornelius Nepos as one of her sons, though the actual town in which he was born has never been satisfactorily determined. Cornelius Nepos was the contemporary and friend of Catullus, who addressed some of his poems to him, and together they passed most of their lives in Rome, where Cicero formed one of their circle.

Æmilius Macer, a well-known poet and philosopher, the friend of Virgil and of Ovid, was also a Veronese. There is a work in verse "treating of the virtues of herbs and of the qualities and instincts of reptiles and birds," by one Macer, but opinions are divided as to whether the author hailed from Verona or was another writer of the same name.

PALAZZO DEL CONSIGLIO.
ARCHITECT FRA GIACONDO.

During the Augustan age in which the above named authors lived, Verona also claimed among her citizens the celebrated architect Vitruvius Cerdone; a claim not always, nor very generally, recognised. His statue however

The Story of Verona

stands among those of her greatest men outside the Palazzo del Consiglio, and perpetuates the fame of the man who designed the once glorious Arco de' Gavi, that arch which formed one of Verona's greatest monuments up till 1805, when it was wantonly taken down. Other writers who were natives of Verona, or of the surrounding province, were Pomponius Secundus (a writer of tragedies, and who, in his capacity of Veronese consul at Rome, gave a great supper to the Emperor Titus, when according to Pliny who was one of the guests, some wine one hundred and sixty years old was drunk); Cassius or Catius Severus; Pliny the Elder, the famous naturalist whose misplaced zeal led him to meet with his death by too close and too curious an investigation of the eruption of Vesuvius, A.D. 81. Pliny the younger, though born at Como, may almost rank as a Veronese. His mother was the elder Pliny's sister, his uncle looked upon him and loved him as his own son, and much of his time was spent at or near Verona.

Verona too was early endowed with a University, or as it was termed in those days, a "Cathedral School." The great impetus given by Charlemagne to public instruction in Italy is one of the traits which redounds most to his honour, and Verona which had always been considered as a spot where learning had met with encouragement, was one of the first towns to profit by the French monarch's generosity. Indeed it is declared that she has done more for Italy with regard to learning than ever Greece or Athens did. This assertion can easily be believed when we read that only nine years after Charlemagne's death an Imperial decree ordained that a public school or college should be founded there, a decree that was endorsed by the Emperor Louis XI. in 824. A bull of Pope Benedict XI. in 1339 sanctions this "University," or more properly, public school, and confirms to it the right of conferring degrees in law, in medicine, and in the arts.

A goodly list could be given of several other writers, many of them bishops and men of saintly lives, whose erudition added to the fame of Verona and spread her renown as a centre of learning into ever-widening circles. Nor were minstrels and troubadours excluded from the list, especially at the beginning of the twelfth century. We read of singers known in the history of minstrelsy, such as Hugues de St Cyr, Pietro Villems, and Sordello, all coming to Verona and finding a welcome there.

All names however pale before that of Dante Alighieri, who, though in no sense a Veronese, found here a haven in his day of adversity and exile, and whose acknowledgment of the hospitality accorded him is of world-wide renown. The causes that brought Dante to Verona have been much discussed. It may be that the strong Ghibelline feelings which predominated in the city made the Florentine exile certain of being understood there—at least as far as his political sentiments were concerned. The renown too possessed by

The Story of Verona

Verona as to the encouragement given within her walls to learning and men of letters may have attracted him. Or more probably still, the knowledge that at the court of the Scaligers he would find not a welcome only, but also a home where his talents would be recognised and appreciated, may have induced him to come to Verona. This last hypothesis may to some extent be borne out by the opening words of the "epistola" written by Dante to Cangrande della Scala at the time he dedicated the *Paradiso* to him. This letter, whose authenticity has given rise to much discussion, but which in these latter times is generally accepted as being his, begins by saying: "I heard the praise of your celebrated magnificence; I came to Verona to assure myself of the same. There I saw your magnanimous doings; I saw, I experienced your benefactions; and while I had at first believed that the fame of them was superior to the deeds, I became convinced that the deeds were superior to the fame."

Dante's choice of Verona was a wise one; and he found there a reception and a refuge that must have soothed to some extent the angry wounded susceptibilities of that "spirito sdegnoso."

The first of the princely house of della Scala to receive Dante was Bartolomeo, who, though he is not mentioned by name by the poet, was without doubt the "grand Lombard" spoken of by Dante's ancestor Cacciaguida in *Paradiso*, canto xvii. 70. For Bartolomeo and Cangrande della Scala Dante has only words of praise; but some other members of their family come in for the full force of the poet's wrath, and he speaks in scathing terms of Alberto and Alboino, the former the predecessor, the latter the successor of Bartolomeo. Nor is he less bitter against an illegitimate son of Alberto della Scala, whom his father had made abbot of S. Zeno, and who exercised that office from 1291 to 1314. Speaking of this deformed priest he says,

" ... in his whole body, sick
And worse in mind, and who was evil born"

(... mal del corpo intero—E della mente peggio, e che mal nacque. *Purg.* xviii. 124, etc.), and how his father "with one foot in the grave" (con un piè dentro la fossa) had "put him in the place of the true pastor" (ha posto in loco di suo pastor vero).

The reason of Dante's dislike for Alboino, who he must have known intimately, has never come to light. The man's want of energy, his indifference as to the Ghibelline cause, his inefficiency as a warrior, may perhaps have aroused that contempt for him which Dante expresses most openly in the *Convito*, iv. 16. Cangrande on the other hand calls forth his admiration; and that Dante dedicated to him the last part of the *Divine Comedy* is proof enough of the esteem and affection in which he held him. Another proof too is forthcoming in the fact adduced by Boccaccio and Giovanni Querini that Dante was wont to send the cantos of the *Paradiso* as he wrote them, and before submitting them to any other eye, to the lord of Verona. The poet recognises too the renown of Cangrande's deeds by putting into the mouth of Cacciaguida the prophecy as to "how notable his works shall be" (che notabile fien l'opere sue); words so concise and so forcible in their depth and truth that they are introduced in the epitaph above Cangrande's tomb in a Latin form.

"Little is known for certain of Dante's actual residence in Verona," says Cipolla; though he quotes from Ampère's *Voyage Dantesque* to show the favourable impression that the town made on this pilgrim not generally prone to be satisfied, nor minded to refrain from a sharp and unfriendly criticism. "Here at last is an Italian city of which Dante has said nothing injurious. She owes this almost unique exception to the hospitality which she offered him."

Dante alludes several times to the town itself in his writings. He speaks so graphically of the game of the Palio (*Inf.* xv. 121) as to make one fancy he must have witnessed it in person. It has been said that his idea of the "bolgie" of the *Inferno* came to him from the shape of the arena at Verona, and that standing on the summit of that vast building he conceived the notion of creating his Hell on the same lines as those presented before his eyes. Whether this is really so or not cannot be definitely affirmed, but it is certain that no other poet has mapped out an Inferno on the same lines as that of Dante, while the form he has given it resembles very closely that of the amphitheatre of Verona.

Other memories than those which spoke to him only of the town were also present to Dante's mind when he was writing his great poem. The country in the heart of the valley of the Adige is depicted by him at the opening of the twelfth canto of the *Inferno*; and the surroundings of the Lake of Garda are spoken of equally in the *Inferno* at canto XX. 64, etc.

It was at Verona that the remarks as to Dante's powers of visiting the Infernal regions first arose. As his "melancholy, pensive" form walked silently through the streets and byeways of the city, the women of the lower classes pointed him out one to another as "he who went to Hell and returned when he listed, and brought news up above of those who were there below." It may be that such unsolicited fame would bring a smile to the solemn, set features, and prove more acceptable than the applause vouchsafed by Cangrande's herd of courtiers.

Another distinguished poet came to Verona in 1348, and indeed visited the town several times. This was no other than Petrarch; and it was on the occasion of his first visit to his friend Guglielmo da Pastrengo that he dreamed the dream which came only too true, of Laura's death (April 6). This does not seem however to have given him a distaste for Verona, where he had many friends, and from where he wrote in ecstasies of the beauty of the Lake of Garda and of the country around.

The wives of the lords of Verona, with but one exception, were not given to literature or the arts. The only one who endeavoured in any way to attract men of letters to her court was Samaritana, wife of Antonio della Scala. This daughter of the house of da Polenta of Ravenna was in reality too vain and frivolous to care for learning for its own sake. She thought it would redound to her glory to collect round her men whose studies or writings would add to the lustre of her name, and for this cause it came to pass that late in the fourteenth century the court of the Scaligers was again frequented by "litterati." The most conspicuous among them was Gidino da Somma Campagna, who dedicated a book entitled *Trattato dei Ritmi Volgari* to Antonio della Scala. The original manuscript of the *Trattato* is preserved in the Biblioteca Capitolare, and the beautiful designs and scrolls that adorn the margins of its pages are an example of the miniature drawing of the day, deserving both of study and admiration. Besides Gidino da Somma Campagna, mention may be made of Leonardo da Quinto, a learned jurisconsult, astrologer, and man of letters. He was, as Guglielmo da Pastrengo had been before him, an ardent bibliophile, and both men were possessed of libraries as fine as any which existed in private houses at that time. When Antonio della

Scala was in straits for money in 1386, Leonardo da Quinto was one of the two emissaries whom he sent to Venice to sell his jewels. Marzagaia and Matteo da Orgiano can also be added to the above literary set; the former was Antonio's tutor; and the latter, really of Vicenza, was a Humanist of high repute who became chancellor at the court of Verona. The possession of a fine library in those days was by no means the privilege of the few. Not only did many of the churches own libraries of no mean order, but most of the private individuals of note in Verona had collections that were at once numerous and costly. The noble houses of Ottolini, Trevisani, Pelligrini, Pindemonte, Moscardo, Maffei, and Muselli had all famous libraries, while English readers will be interested to learn that the great Ashburnham collection had its origin in Verona. This collection was begun by the Marchese Giovanni Saibante of Verona, who devoted many years of arduous and loving devotion to the formation of this unique library. In 1734 it contained 5189 volumes, and 1321 manuscripts, of which 102 were Greek and 70 were Hebrew. The larger part of this collection was sold in Paris; from there it passed into the Earl of Ashburnham's hands, and in 1884 the Italian Government bought it back for the sum of £23,000.

To set down here the names of the Veronese whose fame in connection with letters has added to the glory of their native land would be beside the mark. Suffice it for the present purpose to mention the following:—Guarino dei Guarini, the student of Greek and of Greek science; Girolamo Fracastoro, whose statue by Danese Cattaneo in the Loggia of the Palazzo del Consiglio, set up only two years after his death, shows how generally his talents were recognised as a poet, a philosopher, and an astronomer; Fra Giocondo, whose fame as an architect was widely spread through France and Italy, and was so great as to leave but little room wherein to speak of him as a writer and a scientist; Giovanni Antonio Panteo, an author of various works in Latin, and a friend of all the learned men of his day; Torello Saraina, whose book *De Origine et amplitudine Urbis Veronæ*, published in folio at Verona in 1540, and printed in 1586, is one of the first histories of Verona both as to date and merit; Onofrio Panvinio, a finished Latin scholar, and an elegant writer on all the Roman remains in his native town; Giulio Cesare Bordoni, surnamed Scaligero, as famous as a doctor as he was as a writer and man of science, who is universally known by the name which he added to his own, and which was taken for the purpose of deluding those who knew no better that he was a descendant of the Scaligers. He was without doubt one of the most learned and scientific men of his age, and was honoured and welcomed in every country in which he set foot.

This list must not draw to its close without including the name of Scipione Maffei, whose work *Verona Illustrata*, in eight volumes, and often consulted in the construction of these pages, is one of the most trustworthy and complete histories of Verona as far as it goes. Other writings by Maffei confirmed his celebrity, and his fellow-citizens gave expression to his merits, and to the esteem and affection in which they held him, when they set up, during his lifetime, his statue in the Piazza de' Signori, where it stands to this day close to the Volto Barbaro. Among modern writers, or rather poets, mention must be made of Girolamo Pompei, Ippolito Pindemonte, and Aleardo Aleardi, all poets of the eighteenth and nineteenth centuries, and all of them belonging to patrician families of Verona. Pompei and Pindemonte were apt translators of the great classic poets of Rome; while Aleardi's muse was attuned to songs of love and patriotism.

The rôle of notable writers and men of letters is by no means exhausted in this list, which has no pretence to do more than give an idea of Verona's chief literary sons, and to raise her renown in the scholastic world, as well as in that of art and history.

The school of painting in Verona dates from the reign of Cangrande. There were it is true paintings and frescoes in the town prior to the Scaligers, but they could not come under the classification of a "school," and are of too remote and uncertain a character to be placed as pertaining to a given date. The patronage bestowed by Cangrande on learning and letters was extended also to painting, and Vasari tells how that "Giotto did some pictures for Messer Cane in his palace; and specially the portrait of that lord." That Giotto came to Verona at the bidding of this greatest of the Scaligers is well known, as it is also known that he worked there to a considerable extent. Nothing remains, however, of his work in the "Big Dog's" Palace; and only small and generally "restored" examples are to be found in a few of the churches.

The influence of Giotto is felt though markedly in Verona, where the strong impetus given to painting by Cangrande developed steadily under the rule of his descendants. A German critic (Jules von Schlosser) has indeed said that Verona at that period was the centre of pictorial art in Northern Italy; and were all else wanting, the wonderful miniature painting of that time testifies in itself to the truth of such a statement.

The actual founder of the Veronese school was Altichiero, born about 1300, and of whom some frescoes are to be seen in the church of St Anastasia, and in that of S. Fermo Maggiore, though on this latter point there is some doubt. Together with Altichiero must be mentioned his friend and contemporary Jacopo d'Avanzo, for they frequently worked together, and their dual work on the same picture is not easy to dissever. It cannot be denied that they were greatly inspired by Giotto but, on the other hand, they were by no means blind followers or even pupils of the Florentine master, for they maintained a character in all ways distinct from him, and portrayed their art in fuller, deeper, richer colouring. They were also superior as draughtsmen, conveying too a greater sense of life and movement in their figures, and presenting all through their work a strong and marked individuality. Both artists can really be studied better at Padua than in their native city where little exists that can give a true idea of their talent.

With them may also be mentioned Martini of Verona; who though inferior to Altichiero and d'Avanzo, lived and worked at the same time, and prepared the way for the far greater Vittor Pisano or Pisanello, who was born at S. Vigilio near the Lake of Garda in 1380. The doubt as to who was Pisanello's master remains unsolved to the present day. Morelli inclines to the opinion that he was a pupil of Altichiero—an opinion not shared by Crowe and Cavalcaselle. He doubtless derived much from a study of Altichiero's work, and from drawing from the antique; but his own personality is revealed in his paintings, and more still in his medals and in his treatment of portraits where he represented his sitters "en profile," and obtained a striking and lasting success from this style of portraiture—till then untried and absolutely original. His skill as a medallist caused him to find patrons in almost every court in Italy and to be welcomed at them all in turn. He worked too in conjunction with Gentile da Fabriano in the Ducal Palace at Venice, decorating and restoring that princely building, and imbibing probably much of Gentile's feeling for finish, colour, and brilliancy. "But it is in Verona," says Mr Selwyn Brinton,[37] "that the best of his work in fresco remains—damaged, almost ruined, but attesting to his vigorous art, to his wonderful grasp of animal life." This latter trait is very marked in Pisanello, and shows that his love of animals, his study of them, as well as of nature in every possible form, was deep and true. He introduces some phase of animal life into most of his pictures, and in the care and finish bestowed on every bird or beast that he sets before us, we feel we have to do with an artist who loves and understands his subject.

MADONNA AND CHILD, VITTOR PISANELLO, MUSEO CIVICO

Pisanello is perhaps even more famous as a medallist than as a painter, and speaking of his medallions, the author quoted above says: "They are a gallery of contemporary portraits, priceless to the student of Renaissance history. Leonello d'Este (who was his special friend and patron), lord of Ferrara, with his strong, ugly face; Cecilia Gonzaga, the delicate, refined head poised on the long swan-like neck; Inigo d'Avalos, Marquis of Pescara; Sigismondo Pandolfo Malatesta, the lord of Rimini, the cultured tyrant, the lover of the fair Isotta degli Atti ...; Filippo Maria Visconti, so conscious of his appearance that he lived hid in secret chambers, the last of the Visconti tyrants, his brocaded cap pressed down on the coarse, heavy face; Alfonso of Aragon, the patron of the Humanists; Gian Francesco Gonzaga, the Marquis of Mantua; Johannes Palæologus, with pointed beard and strange Eastern head attire—all these move before us; names of which Italian history is full, and show in the living bronzes their very life and character. And, lastly, the artist himself, a strong, good-tempered, square-set face, clean shaved and cap on head, his broidered jacket just showing; he is proud of his position as painter, and inscribes almost every medal—'Opus Pisani Pictoris.' "[38]

Pisanello was followed by pupils, who though never attaining to their master's height, were good painters, and have left some beautiful and valuable work in the churches and gallery of Verona. The chief of these were Stefano da Zevio (born 1393); Giovanni Oriolo; Giovanni Badile; Girolamo, and Francesco Benaglio. In these painters the feeling for religious art as interpreted from the Veronese point of view was maturing ever more and more till it reached its consummation in the works of Francesco Morone; Girolamo dai Libri; Paolo Morando or Cavazzola; Liberale da Verona; and in those of Liberale's great pupils: Francesco Bonsignori; Gian Francesco Caroto; Francesco Torbido; and Domenico del Riccio, or Brusasorci.

Francesco Morone, the son of Domenico Morone, surnamed Pelacani (dogskinner) himself a painter of considerable merit, was born at Verona in 1473. His work bears the impress of deep religious feeling, rendered always with marvellous sweetness and refinement, and set in tones of fine rich colouring. His frescoes in the Sacristy of Sta. Maria in Organo are declared by Vasari to be among the most beautiful in Italy. In the same church stands his famous Madonna and Child, with S. Augustine and S. Martin below; a very beautiful composition, with its graceful details of canopy flowers and angels. Morone, who died at Verona in 1529, is best studied in his native town, though examples of his work are to be found in the Brera at Milan, and in the National Gallery in London.

Girolamo dai Libri, born at Verona in 1474, was a friend of Morone and a fellow-worker with him at Sta. Maria in Organo. He was brought up, as his father had been before him and as his son was after him, as a miniaturist. This art followed by three generations gave its name to the family, and this surname "of the books" might well be assumed by those whose work had lain so constantly among them. Girolamo's pictures often abound with fruits, flowers, festoons, and backgrounds with architectural details, while through them all runs the soft rich colouring peculiar to the Veronese school and which was inspired largely by the great miniature painters who helped to form that school. The faces in his pictures breathe a spirit of glad yet sober serenity, and the finished detail of trellis-work, lemon trees heavy with their golden fruit, and blossoming flowers which often surround the Madonna and Child bear witness to the training and taste of a skilled miniaturist. Many of his miniatures are in the Picture Gallery of Verona, where there are besides several of his pictures, others being in the churches of that town, others in London, in Berlin, and at Hamilton Palace in Scotland. Girolamo dai Libri died in 1556.

MADONNA, SS. ZENO AND LORENZO GUISTINIANI,
GIROLAMO DAI LIBRI
CHURCH OF ST GEORGE IN BRAIDA

Liberale da Verona, born in Verona in 1451, was like Girolamo dai Libri educated as a miniaturist. Endowed perhaps with greater power than Girolamo he does not always possess such poetic feeling, nor is his colouring so

The Story of Verona

harmonious and pleasant. His manner however underwent a marked change when he came under the influence of Andrea Mantegna. A broader and more forcible tone of feeling then makes itself apparent, and though intense finish and detail are still evident they are subservient to the subject represented in the picture, and in no way detract from the grand lines and colours that now employ his brush. The greater number of his paintings are to be found at Verona; but there is a grand S. Sebastian—perhaps his masterpiece—in the Brera, and other works by him in London, in several towns in Germany, and at Vienna. Liberale had also the merit of forming a goodly array of followers or pupils, whose talents carried on to all time the fame and honour of their master.

Before enlarging on them however it would be well to pause for a moment to speak of Paolo Morando, better known as Cavazzola, who was absolutely distinct from Liberale and Girolamo dai Libri, though living and working at the same time and in the same city. He was born at Verona in 1486, and died when only thirty-six years old. His early death cut short a career of great promise, for Cavazzola had little in common with the simple grave manner of the early Veronese masters, he moved along lines of his own creating, and showed as Burckhardt says in speaking of him a "transition from the realism of the fifteenth century to the noble free character of the sixteenth." As a colourist Cavazzola is cold and hard; and though his tints are glowing as to brilliancy there is little in them that delights the eye or excites pathos or devotion. His drawing though is vigorous, his touch free, untrammelled and broad, with a power and grasp of treatment that caused his contemporaries to speak of him as the Veronese Raphael. Very fine are a series of his pictures, five in number, which treat of the Passion of our Lord in the gallery at Verona. There is in them a serious conception as to composition and vigour in the technique that cause one to realise a master's thought and execution, and to feel what possibilities lay within his grasp when death cut short his career. Nearly all Cavazzola's work is in Verona, though the National Gallery possesses two examples, and one is to be found at Dresden.

To return to Liberale's pupils, Francesco Bonsignori, also called Francesco da Verona, is one of the first, being born at Verona in 1455. His early education, begun in his native town, was continued at Mantua, where he was patronised by the Gonzaghi, and where Mantegna's influence developed his style considerably. He is chiefly known as a portrait painter, a fact that impressed Cosmo Monkhouse, who, ignoring or forgetting Torbido's work in the same direction, speaks thus of Bonsignori: "At Verona, alone almost of all the cities of Italy, there seems to have been little demand for portraits. It produced no portrait painter of eminence, and though the fact does not prove much, it may be noted that the only fine portrait by a Veronese in the National Gallery (that by Bonsignori), is of a Venetian Senator."

Most of his work is at Verona, though some is in Florence, some at Milan, and as already stated one fine portrait is in London. Crowe and Cavalcaselle's criticism on Bonsignori is as follows: "We are reminded of Masaccio by the breadth of the modelling, of Ghirlandajo by the precision of form, of Mantegna there is no trace." This judgment, slightly modified at the close, is endorsed by Morelli who says: "Let anyone study the signed work of Bonsignori (in the churches of S. Fermo, S. Bernardino, S. Paolo and the Municipal Gallery of Verona), and I have no doubt that every connoisseur will see therein the influence of Gian Bellini, and of Alvise Vivarini, but certainly not of Mantegna. Later, no doubt, when at Mantua, Bonsignori learned a good deal from his great colleague." Bonsignori died at Mantua in 1519.

Gian Francesco Caroto, another of Liberale's pupils though influenced besides by Fr. Morone and Mantegna, was born in 1470. He is a delightful and graceful painter, recalling Luini at times; and Morelli speaking of his early works (cir. 1500) writes thus: "The student of the early works of Caroto in the galleries of Modena, of Maldura at Padua, and at Frankfort, will admit that these small Madonnas of his in drawing and modelling recall quite as much his master Liberale as Mantegna."

Caroto is a forcible and striking master; his colouring is warm and soft and harmonious, his drawing powerful. To show in what category his pictures were ranked it is enough to relate how the fine Madonna and Child with angels carrying large lilies, by him at Dresden was received at that gallery with a forged signature of Leonardo. It passed as such for years, though Morelli first, and now the director of the gallery have restored it to Caroto. Selwyn Brinton considers this picture to be "one of the loveliest paintings which all Italian art has bequeathed to us."[39]

Some traces of his fresco painting may yet be seen on the exterior of several Veronese palaces, especially in the neighbourhood of St Thomas of Canterbury, but much of that style of decoration—in which Liberale and Morone also delighted—has perished beneath the ravages of time. In common with the majority of his colleagues, the greater part of Caroto's paintings exist at Verona (his masterpiece there being at S. Fermo), while Modena, Padua, Frankfort, Dresden and London all possess examples of his skill. Gian Francesco had a brother Giovanni Caroto, who was not only a painter but also an engraver. He is though very inferior to his brother.

Francesco Torbido, surnamed Il Moro, is no whit inferior to Liberale's other pupils. Vasari has it that Torbido went first to Venice to study under Giorgione, but that master and pupil did not get on together. From words they

The Story of Verona

came to blows, and Torbido left Venice, and at the same time abandoned his art. He withdrew to Verona, where Liberale not only persuaded him to resume his brush, but he taught him, loved him, and finally made him his heir. His time in Venice had not however been fruitless. Torbido combines a Giorgionesque feeling in his paintings that has sometimes led his work to be ascribed to the great master himself. He maintains at the same time the Veronese manner which he knows how to blend in a most effective way with the Venetian, or as Crowe and Cavalcaselle expresses it, "the double character of Venetian art engrafted on the Veronese." The much discussed portrait in the Uffizi Gallery at Florence, called alternately a "Knight of Malta," and "Gattamelata and his Esquire," and assigned generally to Giorgione, is pronounced by the art-critics cited above as the unmistakable work of Torbido. These same critics say: "This is the unmistakable work of Torbido, illustrated by his strong and unmannered outline, effective enough in chiaroscuro, but sharp in contrast of tints ... wanting the power and modulation of the Venetian." That this portrait hails from Verona there can be little doubt, for besides Torbido, it has sometimes been put down to Caroto, while Morelli assigns it to another and less famous pupil of Liberale, Michele da Verona. Morelli though states that Torbido has not received his lawful meed of praise from Vasari and later writers, and speaks of him as "a personality that deserves to be more closely studied." He recognises how Torbido was influenced by Giorgione and the elder Bonifazio, but adds, that in spite of all "he remained faithful to his first master, Liberale."

The last of Liberale's greater pupils is Domenico del Riccio, whose quaint surname of Brusasorci (burner of rats) has so far met with no explanation. This artist's love of rich glowing colour, of pageants, of gorgeous robes and draperies was ever leading the way—soon to be followed by Paolo Veronese—to the fusion of the art of Verona into that of Venice. His paintings are nearly all at Verona, where the most celebrated is the great fresco in the Palazzo Ridolfi, which has for its subject the meeting of the Emperor Charles V. with Pope Clement VII. at Bologna in 1530. Lanzi, speaking of this painting, says: "One could not see a finer sight.... A great mass of people, effective grouping of figures, animated faces, beautiful movements of men and of horses, variety of raiment, pomp, splendour, dignity, and the joyousness befitting the occasion."

A drawing that Morelli considers to have been the preparatory sketch for this fresco is in red chalk in the Dresden Gallery, and with regard to it he remarks: "Before this drawing one easily discovers how many things Paolo Veronese may have learned from his elder countryman."

Domenico had a son, Felice Brusasorci, of whom several paintings exist in the churches of Verona, and some are also in Milan and at the Louvre; but he is inferior to his father who was at the same time his master.

A short account must be given of a few of Liberale's lesser pupils, who while far from equalling those already mentioned yet deserve to be included among the painters of the Veronese school. One of these is Giovanni Maria Falconetto, whose love of architecture is apparent in nearly all his pictures, for he introduces buildings wherever it is possible to do so, bestowing ever much care on this evident labour of love. He lived to a good old age, and as years drew on he renounced painting and became an architect.

Niccolŏ and Paolo Giolfino, who were brothers were also Liberale's pupils. They were friends of Mantegna who lodged with Niccolŏ (the elder brother and the better painter) when he came to Verona, and decorated the exterior of the house (close to the Porta de' Borsari) with frescoes, few of which have withstood the ravages of time.

Paolo Farinato and Antonio Badile, though influenced by Liberale were not under his tutelage, but they belonged to the great school which he founded, and they helped to the best of their ability to carry it on worthily. Farinato can generally be recognised by the snail which he introduces into his pictures, and which he would seem to adopt as his badge. Badile's glory lies almost exclusively in having been the uncle and master of Paolo Cagliari, surnamed "Il Veronese." This great genius belongs so absolutely to Venice, where he lived and worked and where all his masterpieces are to be found, that he cannot be included in the Veronese school of painting. His surname though reminds everyone that Verona gave him birth, and that he himself was proud to own his sonship, and to subscribe himself to all time as "Paul of Verona."

Speaking of the Veronese school Layard says of it: "No school in Italy, except the Florentine, shows so regular and uninterrupted a development, and none is consequently more deserving of the attention of the student who seeks in art a phase of the human intellect, influenced by local and special circumstances. Nowhere can this school be better studied and understood than in the public gallery and churches of Verona."[40]

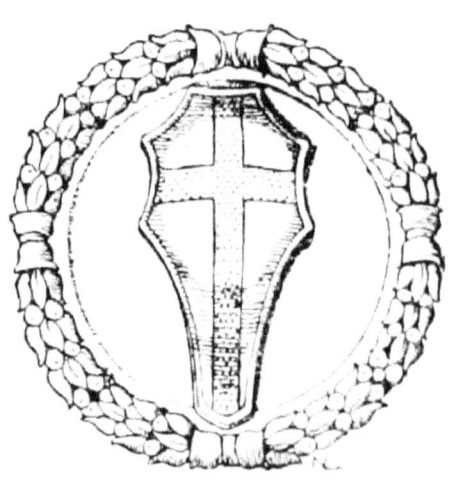

THE ARMS OF VERONA

CHAPTER VII

The Duomo—S. Giovanni in Fonte—Biblioteca Capitolare—Vescovado—St Anastasia—Piazza delle Erbe

The cathedral church of Verona is said to date from between the eighth and ninth centuries. The period of its erection cannot be stated with certainty, and beyond the fact that it was first dedicated to Sta. Maria Matricolata nothing definite relating to it can be affirmed. It was nearly completed in its primitive state in 806 under Bishop Rathold, though it was considerably heightened in after years. The building itself is a mixture of the Lombard style with Gothic and Italian introduced—a mixture eminently satisfactory in its results notwithstanding the divergence of style. Ruskin speaks of it as follows, when, after six months' close study of Byzantine work in Venice, he came again to the Lombard work of Verona and Pavia. "(Verona)—Comparing the arabesque and sculpture of the Duomo here with St Mark's, the first thing that strikes one is the low relief, the second the greater motion and spirit, with infinitely less grace and science. With the Byzantines, however rude the cutting, every line is lovely, and the animals or men are placed in any attitudes which secure ornamental effect, sometimes impossible ones, always severe, restrained, or languid. With the Romanesque workmen all the figures show the effort (often successful) to express energetic action; hunting chiefly, much fighting, and both spirited; some of the dogs running capitally, straining to it, and the knights hitting hard, while yet the faces and drawing are in the last degree barbarous ... the Lombard building is as sharp, precise and accurate as that of St Mark's is careless. The Byzantines seem to have been too lazy to have put their stones together; and, in general, my first impression on coming to Verona, after four months in Venice, is of the exquisitely neat masonry and perfect *feeling* here; a style of Gothic formed by a combination of Lombard surface ornament with Pisan Gothic, than which nothing can possibly be more chaste, pure, or solemn."[41]

A temple dedicated to Minerva is said to have stood here originally, and traces of this can yet be seen, though in point of size there is no difference whatever between the Pagan temple of the past and the Christian church of to-day. The outside decoration of the apses is very beautiful, and is formed of a frieze of carved and decorated work running along the upper lines, and giving an idea of care and finish to the exterior that is very effective. The chief entrance in some ways recalls that of St Zeno. It consists of a beautiful canopied porch, with two columns resting on colossal griffins, while around are scrolls, and carvings, and devices, not of such interesting workmanship as those at St Zeno, though from some lines on the archivolt they claim to be the work of the same man, one Niccolŏ of the eleventh century. Those lines are as follows:—

"Artificem quarum qui sculpserit haec Nicolaum
Hunc concurrentes laudent per saecula gentes."[42]

SOUTH DOOR OF THE DUOMO

On each side of the door, and close to it, stand the figures of Roland and Oliver, the paladins of the Carlovingian age, who stamp alike their romance and epoch in lasting forms of stone on the grand façade of the Duomo of Verona. Around them are grouped Old Testament saints, while in the architrave above are the medallions of three crowned women, who were once supposed to represent Faith, Hope and Charity. They are however three queens who gave generously to the church, namely Bertranda, Charlemagne's mother; one of his wives; and Ermengarda, the wife of Desiderio, the last of the Lombard kings. The façade, with its rows of small columns set so as to show to advantage the noble proportions of the building, is very impressive, and it is interesting to follow the traceries of former windows and speculate over the effect which this west front was once intended to have shown.

The lateral door on the south side is wonderfully fine, and belongs to the earlier and purer date of the building. The polychrome marbles about this doorway prepare the eye for some frescoes of a very early date in the lunette above, while yet higher up and of a still earlier date is a statuette of the Virgin, which may rank as one of the finest of that period in Verona.

The interior of the Duomo is Gothic in its character, and is a very good example of how that style of architecture was then treated in Italy. The ceiling is ugly in its mistaken intention to represent "the starry firmament on high" here set forth in a painted blue curtain meant for the vault of Heaven with gilt stars upon it. The shape of the building is cruciform, and supported by columns and capitals of different forms all made of marble either from Verona or from the East. In the first altar to the left on entering is a picture by Titian of the Assumption. It is a grand painting, and has evidently gained a certain value in the eyes of the Veronese by having been carried off to Paris by Napoleon I., and restored to Verona after that grand pilferer had left Europe and most of his selected goods behind him. The frescoes above the high altar were designed by Giulio Romano, and executed by Torbido in 1534. The rounded colonnaded screen in front of the high altar forms one of the chief features of the church and is extremely beautiful in its way. It was designed by San Micheli, but is not altogether in keeping with its Gothic surroundings, being essentially classic in its plan and execution.

The Story of Verona

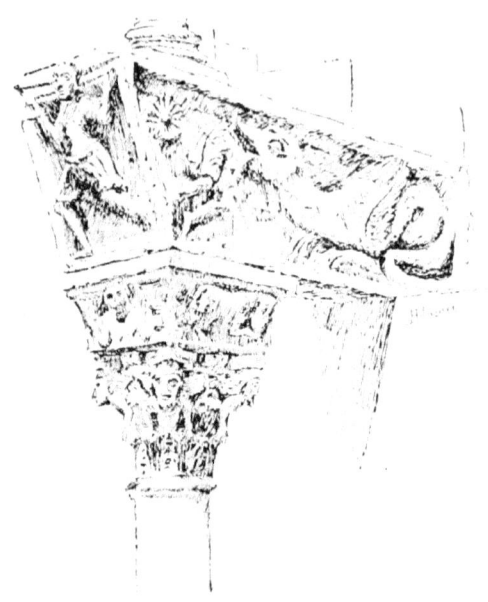

SIDE DOOR OF CATHEDRAL, VERONA.
DETAIL OF COLUMN

On the top of the screen is a beautiful bronze crucifix by Giambattista da Verona, whereon are the arms of Bishop Ludovico Canossa, in whose episcopate it was set up. There is evidently some fine work both as to marbles and paintings on the altar immediately to the proper right of the high altar, but an ugly, modern erection (said to be temporary) in front of the organ shuts out all the light and leaves the fancy free to speculate over glories that perhaps do not exist. The organ itself, a good specimen of "barocco" work, is richly decorated, and its doors are painted by Felice Brusasorci. Close to it, but lost and hidden by the stand above mentioned, is the Cappella Maffei, with some good, though small paintings by Francesco Morone; and some frescoes by Falconetto— indeed the best work done by this latter, signed by him and bearing the date 1503, is to be found among these frescoes.

The altar beyond the high altar and to its proper left, is known as that of St Agatha (1353), and contains a lovely tomb partly Gothic, partly Renaissance. A few of the bones of the saint are buried here, the rest are interred at Catania. Below these relics again lies the body of Sta. Maria Consolatrice, a sister of St Annone (bishop of Verona in the fourth century), who was brought here in 1807 when the church which was named after her, and where till then her body had rested, was suppressed.

The last altar to the left coming out of the church contains part of a picture by Liberale having for its subject the Adoration of the Magi. Mr Selwyn Brinton says of this picture: "He (Liberale) was living between 1489 and 1490 in Verona, when he painted the Adoration of the Kings in the Duomo, with a rich landscape. Here he is still the miniaturist in feeling; his drawing careful, but unsound; his action quaint and startling; his bright colours thrown together without harmony; his background exuberant in detail."[43]

Leaving the church by a small door in the left hand corner we come into all that is left of the first church of Sta. Maria Matricolare, from which the cathedral actually took its name and which it retained till it was sunk in that of Duomo. The remains of this church consist now of only six columns with capitals of Lombardo-Byzantine style; and from here we pass into the adjoining small church of S. Giovanni in Fonte, which served in past times as the Baptistery. It has a magnificent octagonal font in the centre, carved out of a single block of Verona marble, on which a series of bas-reliefs, well worth studying, represent in humorous and quaintly primitive carving scenes from the early life of our Lord. Within the octagonal font is a smaller one in quatrefoil shape, wherein the priest was wont to stand and submerge the catechumens who presented themselves for baptism. A painting by Paolo Farinato, representing the baptism of Christ, stood formerly over the high altar, but has now been moved to a side wall, where other works by Giovanni Caroto, Falconetto, and an unknown pupil of Brusasorci, are all hung—and hung too high. Falconetto's picture is an extremely fine one, recalling in composition, feeling and colouring—at least, as far as can be made out at such a distance—the school of Gian Bellini and the great early Venetian masters.

From the little church of S. Giovanni in Fonte we turn away to the left, and keeping always in that direction, having gone round a corner or two, we reach the cloisters of the cathedral. They recall in some way those of St Zeno, though not altogether similar in arrangement. Here the bases and capitals are united, each pair as at St Zeno being cut out of a single block, while on the side nearest the church the pillars are double—an effect that is remarkably beautiful and striking.

DETAIL OF SIDE DOOR OF DUOMO, VERONA

The Duomo forms a centre around which clusters much that is interesting, though the time for investigating these various sights will not in reality take long. In the Piazza on the left hand side facing the chief portal stands the Biblioteca Capitolare, a library belonging to the Duomo, and containing some 18,000 volumes in all. The date of some of the treasures contained here is what constitutes the value of this library, and enhances its worth and interest to an untold extent. It is said to be even superior to the Vatican as to the number of the old codexes which it possesses; and which—not including fragments of the fourth century—date from the fifth to the ninth centuries. It was here that Petrarch discovered the letters of Cicero. Niebuhr brought to light the institutions of Gaius, compiled in the reign of Caracalla; and men of letters of all nations and languages find scope here for research and labour. The value of these codexes is incalculable. The greater part are membranous, many of them being palimpsests, others being written in purple having the sacred names inscribed in gold and silver, and all of them offering fields of discovery whereof students (many from England but more still from Germany) are not slow to take advantage. This library contains besides treasures of varied sorts, for here may be seen the baptismal certificate of Prince Charles Edward, the young pretender, dated "Roma, ultima Dicemb. 1720." A most friendly and learned custodian, Don Antonio Spagnolo, is only too pleased to show the treasures committed to his charge and to explain everything relating to his priceless and loved books to all who are interested in such matters.

Opposite this library stands the old disused church of S. Pietro in Cattedra, with a statue of St Peter over the doorway, and some graceful windows of the cusped arched order belonging to the fourteenth century. Close to the Duomo again is the church of St Elena, containing some pictures by Falconetto, Felice Brusasorci, and Niccolŏ da Verona; but the chief interest attaching to this church is the tradition that Dante held here the conference in Latin in which he treated "of the elements of earth and water" (De duobus elementis terrae et acquae); if indeed that much disputed treatise is by him, a point much questioned in these days.

Passing round by the east front of the Duomo, and gazing again with admiration on the frieze running round the apse, a work which speaks so plainly of an earlier date than the interior of the church, we come to the Vescovado, or the Bishop's Palace. This has been altered and rebuilt at various epochs, chiefly about the year 1356; and within its walls Bishop Ognibene received Pope Lucius III. who died here in 1185 when his successor Urban III. was immediately named in his stead. The doorway leading to the palace is a very beautiful bit of work, having the date MD.II. inscribed on it and said to be by Fra Giocondo of Verona. It is of a later date than the walls which support it on either side; and leads in its turn into a striking courtyard with columns and arches of the fanciful Cinquecento style. Inside the Episcopal Palace there is a beautiful predella in the chapel by Liberale consisting of three paintings which represent the Adoration of the Magi, the Nativity of our Lord, and the passing of the Blessed Virgin. There is also said to be a picture by Caroto in the palace, but this is kept in a room not generally shown to visitors.

CHURCH OF ST ANASTASIA FROM THE ADIGE SHEWING THE HOUSES WHICH STOOD THERE BEFORE THE *muraglioni*, BUILT TO DEFEND THE TOWN AGAINST THE INUNDATIONS OF THE ADIGE, WERE ERECTED

Several palaces belonging to the old patrician families of Verona are to be found in the neighbourhood of the Duomo. In the Via Pigna stands the Palazzo Miniscalchi, the work of the great architect Michele San Micheli, and adorned externally with frescoes. These latter which have suffered outrageously at the hands of would-be restorers were originally by Torbido, and ranked as some of the best work he ever did in that way. The rest are by Giambattista Zeloti.

Not far from the Duomo stands the church of St Anastasia, a church that owes its being to the Dominicans, to Guglielmo da Castelbarco, to Alberto della Scala, and to Pietro Scaligero, bishop of Verona. This church is a beautiful example of the brick and marble work that abounds to such a remarkable extent in Verona, and dates from the second half of the thirteenth century. The façade of unfinished brickwork is rich in mouldings and decorations—equally of brick—and sets off the fine portal which leads into the church, and which is bilateral. The great wooden double doors are very fine, and the carvings in marble, together with the frescoes in the lunettes above, give a sense of great richness and finish to this principal entrance of the church, in spite of the incomplete condition of the façade. The original plan was evidently to have faced it all with slabs of marble, or more probably with panels in relief, to some extent no doubt like those now seen at the side representing scenes from the life of St Peter Martyr. These latter however are of a later date than the brickwork of the façade, as is also the Renaissance ornamentation round the doors.

*HOLY WATER BASIN IN ST ANASTASIA
FIGURE CARVED BY GABRIEL CAGLIARI, FATHER OF
PAUL VERONESE*

The interior is dignified and fine, consisting of a nave and two narrow side aisles, separated by twelve columns, and terminating in an apse of five divisions. The eye is at once caught, though not perhaps attracted, on entering by the holy water stoups, which consist of two humpbacked figures, grotesque in the extreme, and that stand one on each side immediately under the two first columns. The one to the left was carved by Gabriel Cagliari, the father of Paolo Veronese; the other on the right is the work of Alessandro Rossi, the father of the humpbacked painter, Giambattista Rossi known as "Gobbino," and on it is inscribed the date of 1591. The Gothic vaulting of the building is fine, and had the frescoes that once covered it but remained to this day, the effect of colour and symmetry (which is striking even now when many of the frescoes have disappeared) would have been enhanced a hundredfold.

Several fine altars are ranged on either side of the church, many of them raised on classic lines; others again being a mixture of classic and Renaissance. The first altar on the right hand side, that of the Fregoso family, is Corinthian, and is reckoned by Vasari as one of the finest in Italy. It was both designed and sculptured in 1565 by Danese Cattaneo. The second altar is adorned with a good deal of "finto bronzo," and is a mixture of Renaissance and classical work that harmonises very happily. High up and hardly to be seen even with glasses is a fresco attributed to Mantegna. It is said to have been "executed with the utmost care"; but no judgment is possible in this case from below. The third altar is again one of those successful blendings of the Renaissance and classical styles, where rich carvings in marble and stone are shown off to untold advantage in their setting of severe lines. Here again we have to take on faith the statements as to some frescoes of Caroto of the date of 1470, though too high up for mortal sight or sense to presume to criticise. There is also here an entombment ascribed to Liberale. The fourth altar is built on the lines of the Arco de' Gavi, and is of interest and service as setting before us, with very slight deviations, a model of that famous arch as it once stood close to Castel Vecchio. This altar was erected by Fiorio Pindemonte in the year 1539, and has a fine picture of St Martin, one of the last works of Gian Francesco Caroto.

The chapel known as that of the Crucifix is particularly interesting. It is entered under a beautiful archway of rich Lombardesque carving in red marble, and over the altar hangs a wooden image of our Lord on the Cross, of a very remote date, and by an unknown artist. On the left facing this crucifix is a most curious painted terra-cotta representation of the Entombment. The expression on the faces of all who are taking part in the sad and sacred task is marvellously given, and is full of character and feeling. Over the next altar belonging to the Centrago family is a picture, in a lovely frame of the same date, of the Madonna and Child, enthroned with St Augustine and St Thomas Aquinas, by Francesco Morone (1474). It is also ascribed sometimes to Girolamo dai Libri. Very beautiful too is the decorative festoon of carved flowers round the altar. The Gothic tomb and the frescoes at the side belong probably to the same family; and no doubt the very attractive old couple whose portraits are at the bottom of the painting were the donors of all in that chapel. This same chapel, which stands in a kind of transept of the church, leads into one of the divisions of the apse where the Cappella Cavalli is. It is decorated with frescoes of a very early date, which have been in turn ascribed to Altichiero, Giotto, Morone, and Liberale, and representing knights of the Cavalli family kneeling before the Virgin and Child, with other warriors in attendance. Below the frescoes is the mausoleum of the knight Federigo Cavalli. There is also here a fine tryptich of our Lord in the centre, with St Jerome on one hand and St Gemignano on the other. In the niches are carved figures, with paintings in between by Liberale.

By the side of the Cavalli chapel stands that of the Pellegrini family, panelled with terra-cotta reliefs, the work of a German, in 1400, whose name is unknown. There is a fine figure of a pilgrim (a play upon the family name, and emblematical of their badge), who kneels in the corner with his hands clasped fast in prayer. The most precious thing in this chapel was a fresco by Pisanello, which fortunately is now being removed from a position where it could not be seen, and, worse still, where it was suffering from damp, to a place of safety in the sacristy. It represents St George about to mount his steed after he has slain the dragon and freed the princess.[44]

*MADONNA AND SAINTS. ST ANASTASIA
ASCRIBED ALTERNATELY TO FRANCESCO MORONE
AND GIROLAMO DAI LIBRI*

On the proper right of the high altar is a large equestrian statue of Cortesia Serego (1432), who was the brother-in-law of Antonio della Scala, and also his general. The florid decorations around the statue are of carved wood. The frescoes round that again are probably by Francesco Bonsignori, while those still higher up are sometimes ascribed to Stefano da Zevio

(1332). The adjoining chapel owned by the Lavagnoli family, though also known as that of St Anna, contains some frescoes, unfortunately much injured, in the style of Mantegna. The next chapel, that of the Salerno family, where there is a fine Gothic monument to Giovanni Salerno, is used as the belfry. What with the mass of hanging ropes, and the storage of church furniture that lumbers up most of this chapel, it is not easy to form a right opinion of some fine old frescoes said to belong to the first half of the fourteenth century, or to do more than lament the bad condition in which they are kept. In the sacristy stands the rescued fresco of St George by Pisanello, and a fine picture by Felice Brusasorci, while outside the sacristy are some frescoes by an unknown hand sadly retouched with startling colours. In the Capella del Rosario is a picture of the Madonna and Child between St Dominic and St Peter Martyr, with the portraits of Mastino II. della Scala and his wife, Taddea da Carrara, kneeling at the base of the picture on either side.

The tradition that once ascribed this picture to Giotto has now been completely done away. The Flagellation here is by Ridolfi. The next chapel, that of the Miniscalchi family, is rich in Renaissance and classical decoration, and possesses a good picture by Giolfino of the Descent of the Holy Spirit (1518).

The remaining altars in the church have no objects that claim any special attention, and after a study of so much that is beautiful and absorbing, it is almost a relief to wander away, noting only once again the glory of the entire church, and observing with pleasure the very effective and simple design of the pavement at our feet in its threefold pattern of grey and red and white marble.

Immediately outside the church on the right hand side stands the tomb of Guglielmo da Castelbarco, the friend and councillor of Cangrande della Scala—and a friend too to Verona, in that it was his largess that contributed chiefly to the building of St Anastasia and of that of S. Fermo as well.

TOMB OF GUGLIELMO DA CASTELBARCO

This munificent patron of Verona (who was besides its Podestà deserved to have what has been justly termed the most perfect monument in the city where the finest monuments existing in Italy are to be found. Ruskin indeed has pronounced it to be, "the most perfect Gothic monument in the world"; and again he alludes to it as "pure and lovely, my most beloved throughout all the length and breadth of Italy—chief as I think among all the sepulchral marbles of a land of mourning."

Four columns of white marble surmounted by sculptured capitals bear the canopy, which is formed of a simple Gothic arch, richly cusped and adorned with a decorative piece of carving in harmony with the purity of style which marks the whole of the monument. Under the canopy lies the effigy of the dead magistrate, a recumbent figure laid on the top of a red marble sarcophagus, which rests in its turn on the backs of two couchant lions. The whole is bound together by bars of iron along whose surface a delicate tracery is outlined. An effect is thus obtained of wonderful strength and grace: for besides the sense of security given by these bars, the eye is carried along their linear decoration to observe still more forcibly the perfect symmetry and proportion of the monument. No name exists as to the author of this masterpiece, but in this case surely it may be asserted that the good he did is not interred with his bones, but that it lives after him, a beauty and a joy for ever.

Three other tombs stand beyond that of Guglielmo da Castelbarco and immediately outside the adjoining church of St Peter Martyr. The first is that of Guinicello

The Story of Verona

de' Principi of a noble family of Bologna, and bears the date of 1273; the next is that of Leonardo da Quinto, the learned jurisconsult alluded to in chapter vi., and one of the witnesses to Cansignorio's will in 1375; the last is to a member of the Dussaimi family. Speaking of these tombs Ruskin says: "Whose they are is of little consequence to the reader or to me, and I have taken no pains to discover; their value being not in any evidence they bear respecting dates, but in their intrinsic merit as examples of composition. Two of them are within the gate, one on the top of it, and this latter is on the whole the best, though all are beautiful; uniting the intense northern energy in their figure sculpture with the most serene classical restraint in their outlines, and unaffected, but masculine simplicity of construction."[45]

The small church of St Peter Martyr close by was once a part of the convent of St Anastasia. It was endowed by the Knights of Brandenburg, whom Cangrande II. summoned to his assistance in 1353, and of whom his special bodyguard was formed. Some of the portraits of these knights can be seen in the paintings of their gracefully proportioned church, which was also enriched by several frescoes, the most remarkable being that of Falconetto above the high altar. This is a strange rendering under symbolical emblems of the Incarnation: the Blessed Virgin being seated in an enclosure with all manner of quaint beasts around her, while the Babe descends from Heaven in a halo of light. A crucifix said to be by Giotto, but of a far earlier date, hangs above Falconetto's painting, and around are other frescoes by Badile. In front of the church of St Anastasia and at the side of that of St Peter Martyr is a statue in white Carrara marble to Paul Veronese; designed by Della Torre and executed by Romeo Cristiani. It was erected in 1888.

PIAZZA DELLE ERBE

The Story of Verona

Following the Corso St Anastasia we come to the Piazza delle Erbe, the market-place of Verona, where chatter and merry gossip together with the sale of flowers, vegetables, plants, owls, birds, and other strange wares go on in as picturesque and original a setting as can be found anywhere. The whole of the Piazza is spread with large white umbrellas, that look like unfinished tents, and that contrast admirably with the sea of colour which flows beneath, and which varies from the many tints worn by the chattering vendors to the hues of the fruits and flowers it behoves them to sell. In the early morning the bustle and stir is at its height; trade is brisker than at any other time, and the life and movement then going on give a character to the place, hardly to be imagined by those who see it for the first time in the afternoon, when the folded umbrellas, the silence and tidiness where all was business and animation, give no real or correct idea of the Piazza. The historical interest which centres round the Piazza delle Erbe is as great as its picturesque attraction. In the days of the Romans the Forum stood here, and the shape of the Piazza is still that of a circus, though the modern houses around have somewhat narrowed the "periferia." Before the Amphitheatre was built it was here that the gladiatorial fights were held. At the northern end stands the column of St Mark, which was placed there as has been said at the period of the League of Cambray at the moment when Verona was restored to the rule of Venice. It is formed of a single block of marble, bearing aloft the winged lion, which represented for so many years the dominion of Venice over the town of Verona. This mark of supremacy, raised in 1524, was destroyed at the moment of "Les Pâques Véronaises" in 1797; but in 1888 it was replaced, no longer as a sign of thraldom or submission but a graceful homage to "the days that are no more." Below the column stands the fountain erected according to some by King Alboin, according to others by King Pepin in 807, and for which Berengarius introduced the water supply in 916. Its use as a fountain was not however really brought about till Cansignorio in 1370 rearranged it on thoroughly working and practical lines. This water supply is probably obtained from one of the great thermae or baths of the Romans, and is surmounted by a statue in Greek marble known as "Madonna Verona." According to an inscription now preserved in the Museo Lapidario this statue was placed in its present position in the days of the Emperor Theodosius (380) by the Consul Valerius Palladio. The motto in "Madonna Verona's" hands is: "est justi latrix urbs haec, et laudis amatrix," and was put there after the peace of Constance in 1183, the year in which Verona was declared free.

A little further down is the Tribune or "Berlina," set up in 1207, from where public decrees were formulated and sentences of death were pronounced. Here too in the days of the Scaligers was the spot where they took their oath of office. The buildings around are for the most part of interest. Immediately to the north of St Mark's column is the Palazzo Trezza (formerly Maffei) a fine block of masonry though of Barocco style—the upper part is very inferior—and containing inside a curious spiral staircase. Close by this palace stands the "Torre del Gardello" set up by Cansignorio, where in 1370 he placed the first clock that struck the hours in Verona. To the left looking down the Piazza, stands the Casa dei Mazzanti, where Albertino della Scala lived (1301), and decorated externally with frescoes by Alberto Cavalli of Mantua in the style of Guilio Romano. On the other side of the Piazza are houses with frescoes by Liberale and Girolamo dai Libri; and beyond them is the old house of merchandise, the Casa dei Mercanti of the year 1301, in red marble, now restored and still used as a Chamber of Commerce. Almost opposite it rises the grand tower of the Lamberti, or as it is sometimes called of the Municipio, to a height of 273 feet. There is hardly a guide-book to Verona that does not say that this tower was built by the Lamberti family; a statement however that has no confirmation in any of the archives or city documents, where no mention of even a family of the name of Lamberti belonging to Verona is to be met with.

CHAPTER VIII

Piazza dei Signori—Sta. Maria Antica—Tombs of the Scaligers

Under the archway known as that of "La Costa," from the thigh bone of some antidiluvian monster which hangs from it, the way leads from the Piazza delle Erbe to the Piazza dei Signori, or Piazza Dante as it is frequently called, a name it takes from a statue of the poet by Ugo Zannoni, placed there in 1865. This Piazza teems with every personal association relating to the Scaligers. Their public and private life centred round this spot; for while it was here that their dwelling-houses were built and their seat of government set up, it was also close by here that the little church of Sta. Maria Antica stood where they worshipped, and beside whose walls are grouped the tombs that glorify them in death.

The Story of Verona

PIAZZA DEI SIGNORI

Entering from the Piazza delle Erbe the first building on the right is the Palazzo della Ragione, now used, as in days of yore, for government offices, and where the traces of old and former windows are still to be seen. On the outside wall a tablet records that "Guglielmo dall'Ossa," a Milanese, being "Podestă of the Comune, this palace known as that Della Ragione was built in 1183 for the public offices." Below this tablet is an archway leading into a courtyard built chiefly of brick and marble, with fine rounded arches all much restored, and from whose midst rises a glorious outer staircase leading to the first floor of the building where an exhibition of modern works of art is kept. The outline of a huge lion of St Mark is to be seen on the outside of the Palazzo della Ragione, which shared the same fate as the one of the column in the Piazza delle Erbe at the moment of "Les Pâques Véronaises." The whole exterior of the palace bears marks of having undergone much restoration, most of which was done in the sixteenth century. Indeed there is not much in this Piazza which has not been repaired or altered at one time or another, and now and again it requires much care and study to make out the original design and material once used for the construction of this historic spot.[46]

The Story of Verona

OUTSIDE STAIRCASE, PUBLICO PALAZZO

It is interesting to compare these two sketches. The first shows the staircase as it stood some four years ago with an upper colonnade of fine "Cinquecento" work. The second shows that work swept away, under the delusion that it was better to see the staircase in its original form.

On the other side of the Via Dante stands the battlemented tower of the Scaligers flanking the Palazzo Tribunalizio, where a tablet states that "Cansignorio della

Scala, Podestă and Captain of the people from December 14, 1359, to October 10, 1375, when he died, built and inhabited this palace, which was remodelled in the sixteenth century into rooms for the Venetian Captaincy." This tower with its forked battlements was at one time a handy prison-house for any who fell under the displeasure of the Scaligers. A doubtful legend runs that no less than four hundred prisoners (one writer says they were only fifty-three) were once confined within its walls, and that to the surprise of all who were not in the secret the whole number died "naturally" in one day! The further statement that they had all died of the same complaint gave a momentary alarm as to an outbreak of the plague, but as no further victims succumbed this alarm also died away.

A doorway by the great architect, San Micheli leads into a courtyard where traces of lovely but fast vanishing frescoes show what glories once reigned around, and remind one that barbarous and cruel in many ways as the rulers of Verona were, they were not indifferent to the beautifying of their town, nor to that patronage of art which rightly or wrongly we associate with a noble nature.

THE OUTSIDE STAIRCASE, PALAZZO
DELLA RAGIONE

On one side of the courtyard are some arches of pointed brick-work supported by stone columns with slightly decorated capitals, a work which was executed under the Venetian rule. Opposite is seen the Porta dei Bombardieri, an ugly erection of stone cannons, drums and implements of war which was set up in 1687. Inside this courtyard is a striking inscription in honour of Zaccaria Barbaro, who was the Podestà appointed by Venice over Verona during the latter half of the fifteenth century. It is recorded of him that he restored three castles in the city and several in the country, as well as changing the prætor's house from wood to stone.

His special claim to admiration, however lies in the fact that at a moment of scarcity of corn "he saw to relieving hunger, that he governed with integrity, administering equal rights to all, so that at the close of his office the people remembered him with tears, 1476."

A way was opened out from this courtyard by the Commune in 1817, so as to give employment to the work people of the town, it being then a time of dire want. This way leads to a small public garden, used as a Botanical School, and that was formerly the garden of Cansignorio della Scala.

The next building of the Scaligers in the Piazza dei Signori is that built by Mastino I. (1272) and where he and his descendants actually lived. It is now used as the Prefettura, and as in the Tribunale Guidiziario (built by Mastino's brother, Alberto), little of the old buildings remain, and less still of the frescoes and decorations that once adorned them. It is known, and has been mentioned, that at Cangrande's orders Giotto decorated much of this home of the Scalas, that portraits of Dante, of Uguccione della Faggiuola, and other illustrious men were drawn by him here. No trace however remains either of his work, or of that of Altichiero who is also said to have worked here, to convey even an idea of what was once to be seen.

The Story of Verona

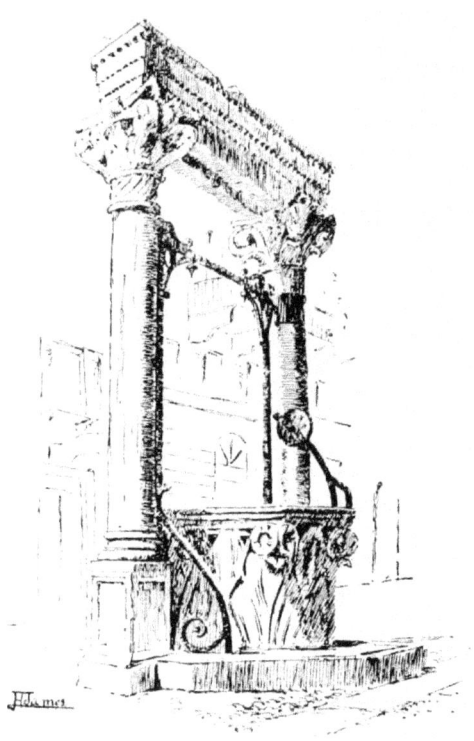

FIFTEENTH CENTURY WELL IN VIA MAZZANTI

At right angles with this former residence of the lords of Verona stands the Palazzo del Consiglio, or old Town hall, more often called La Loggia di Fra Giocondo, though critics are not agreed as to whether he designed the Loggia or whether it is the work of Antonio Riccio, or Rizzo, a Veronese. It is generally attributed to Fra Giocondo, and is a most perfect and beautiful example of Renaissance style. It was erected by order of the Venetian Republic in 1497, and is reckoned as one of the loveliest buildings of that time in the North of Italy. It is a pity that a good deal of unnecessary gilding was added in 1873 when the building underwent some restoration. High up on the corner pillar to the left is to be seen a figure in a monk's dress, which without sufficient warrant is accepted as that of Fra Giocondo; while above are statues of the men who by their learning or deeds have brought celebrity to themselves and to Verona—Catullus; Cornelius Nepos; Pliny the younger; Vitruvius Cerdo; and others. Within the Loggia are two figures in bronze by Girolamo Campagna, which formerly stood outside and which represent the Annunciation. Around are busts of men who have deserved well of their town in modern days. The original design to carry on the Renaissance work of this Palace all along the same side of the square was never fulfilled, and the archway which carries on its topmost height a statue of Fracastoro, the eminent poet and physician, closes the line of marked and beautiful architecture. The building on the other side of this beautiful archway leads to another archway in brick over which is a statue of the Marchese Scipione Maffei, the historian (d. 1755). Passing under this archway into the Via Mazzanti is a lovely old fountain bearing the date of 1478 on the architrave. It is composed chiefly of the red marble from Sant' Ambrogio (a few miles outside Verona), and is as good and perfect a specimen of its kind as can be seen anywhere. Almost opposite this fountain or well in the Via Rosa is a strange Latin inscription which records an important gift to the town by a member of the grand old Roman family de' Gavi. It tells how this noble patrician brought an acqueduct through Verona right over to the left bank of the Adige; an undertaking for which he had to pay the sum of 500,000 sertices. A noble and generous gift when we reflect that such a sum would nowadays represent some £5000. Between the Volto Barbaro and the Via la Costa is a fine brick building, now much defaced by decorations of the seventeenth century. It was originally designed in 1273 as a palace for "i Giudici assessori," but an earthquake in 1511 partly ruined it and modern alterations have reduced it to its present condition.

Crossing the Piazza again past the Palace of the Tribunes, we come at once to the church of St Maria Antica and the Tombs of the Scaligers. It is well to enter for a moment into the small, dim Lombardic church of St Maria Antica, the church used by the Scaligers as their private chapel, and around which they elected to have their burial ground. The church was built originally by the monks of St Oliveto, and dates from about the year 1000. Its restoration done in recent times, though it has left probably little of the original building, has been carried out with taste and judgment. The stern, simple lines of the arches, the stone capitals and pillars are effective and dignified, and act as a fitting preparation for the grand monuments which stand outside, and which merit the closest study. The first is that of Francesco della Scala, better known as Cangrande, whose rule as sole lord after his brother Albono's death lasted from 1311 to 1329. His monument stands over the entrance to the church, and is surmounted by a gracefully cusped canopy, on the top of which is placed an equestrian statue of the greatest of the Della Scala family. A marble sarcophagus rests under the canopy, upheld by four lovely columns with Corinthian capitals, and on the sarcophagus is stretched a recumbent figure of Cangrande, "with hands clasped fast as if still in prayer." His effigy above on horseback is that of a knight in armour; his horse clad too for battle. He holds a huge sword in his hand, his helm is flung far back behind his shoulders. The rider turns his face towards you and smiles, an indication it may be that Death, for whom he had no fear while yet in this life, has equally no dread for him now that he is to meet him face to face. The tomb rests on the figures of two great mastiffs, apt emblems of the "Cangrande" who sleeps above, and who support with doglike fidelity the shields emblazoned with ladders (*scala*) committed to their charge.

EFFIGY OF CANGRANDE

The other tombs all stand in a piece of enclosed ground round the church, and are fenced in with a railing of beautiful wrought ironwork, buckled together so as to be shaken easily by the hand, and adorned at every point with the family device of the ladder. The first tomb inside this small cemetery is that of Mastino I., the founder of the family, who rests under a plain marble sarcophagus, whereon is carved a cross, and where are engraved not only the Scala arms, but those too of Antonio Nogarola, who was with Mastino at the moment when he was assassinated, and who shared the same fate, and evidently the same grave. Beyond that is the tomb of Mastino's brother, Alberto I., who died in 1301. This too is of red marble, but much more ornamented than the first, where besides a relief of Alberto kneeling before the Blessed Virgin, are other reliefs of palm branches, heraldic devices, griffins, birds, and so forth. But the monuments which claim especial attention after that of Cangrande I., are those of Mastino II., and of his son Consignorio. These are likewise formed of three stories, having the equestrian statue above the apex, and the recumbent figure laid upon the sarcophagus. Each however is in its turn more decorated, richer in design and carving, and more elaborate both as to conception and execution than that of the "Great Dog." The tomb of Mastino II. is by one Perino of Milan, and the bold, fine way in which the architect has planned and carried out his work proves him to have been a master of his art. His plan of placing the pyramid or apex with the horse and his rider on the four pillars of Verona marble is very striking; while the perfect way in which these shafts bear the weight laid on them is a model of skill and of beauty. On the façades of the arches are high reliefs representing Old Testament characters; and the bas-reliefs on the stone coffin are equally taken from Old Testament stories. Mastino is shown with his vizor drawn and his features completely hidden from view. As has been seen in Mastino's history, his actions were not always honourable, nor his expeditions always successful.

The legend (alluded to in chapter iv.) as to his never having shown his face again, even to his wife Taddea da Carrara, after the murder of the bishop Bartolomeo della Scala (1338), would seem to have taken shape in his monument, and his desire as to concealing his features even after death was evidently respected to the end.

MONUMENT OF GIOVANNI DELLA SCALA, VERONA

In the north-east corner of the little cemetery stands the most gorgeous of the Scaliger tombs. It is that of Cansignorio, and was raised by him during his lifetime, the architect and sculptor being Bonino da Campiglione. This monument far exceeds that of Cangrande I. and Mastino II. in exuberance of ornamentation and in richness of detail. Cansignorio was evidently determined to atone for the lack of godliness and goodness in his nature by an ostentatious display of saintly characters and saintly actions about his tomb. As has been shown, he was cunning, ambitious, and cruel, and a fratricide twice told. He had nevertheless no hesitation in causing himself to be represented as being received by our Lord and His mother in an attitude of devotion, and probably had no misgivings as to the eventful fulfilment of the scene thus given. The monument is hexagonal, supported on six columns; the canopy and apex are of Verona marble, of the kind known as "mandolato," while the inside dome of the canopy is painted with gold stars on a blue ground. Six figures of warrior saints on square pilasters keep watch over this lord of Verona (who some writers say was neither a saint nor a warrior) and are St Quirinus, St Valentine, St George, St Sigismund, St Martin, and St Louis. Above them again are the figures of Faith, Hope, Charity, Prudence, Justice, and Fortitude; while to crown the whole is the effigy of Cansignorio himself on horseback, with his vizor raised and the "scala" on his breast. This badge of the family is brought in at every possible opportunity, and is always here shown surmounted by the Cross.

The Story of Verona

TOMB OF CANSIGNORIO DELLA SCALA

Very beautiful also is the tomb of Giovanni della Scala, an illegitimate member of the family, and Vicar-General of Vicenza. His remains, first buried in the church of St Fermo Minore, were afterwards brought here, and laid to rest with every honour, and in a manner befitting such impressive surroundings. These monuments are Gothic in style, and may justly rank among the finest things that the fourteenth century has produced in this way. It must be borne in mind that they were fashioned before Verrocchio and Donatello had executed the works which were to astonish the world, and model for after generations the types of equestrian statues which were to serve as guides for all ages to come. It will be well to refresh our memories with Ruskin's beautiful words as to these tombs, words which were poured forth in all the glow of admiration and enthusiasm over objects he loved so well, and which he describes in language which cannot be heard too often.

"At Verona, where the great Pisan school had strong influence, the monumental sculpture is immeasurably finer than at Venice; and so early as about the year 1335, the consummate form of the Gothic tomb occurs in the monument of Cangrande della Scala at Verona. It is set over the portal of the chapel anciently belonging to the family. The sarcophagus is sculptured with shallow bas-reliefs representing (which is rare in the tombs with which I am acquainted in Italy, unless they are those of saints), the principal achievements of the warrior's life, especially the siege of Vicenza and battle of Piacenza; these sculptures, however, form little more than a chased and roughened groundwork for the fully relieved statues representing the Annunciation, projecting boldly from the front of the sarcophagus. Above, the lord of Verona is laid in his long robe of civil dignity, wearing the simple bonnet, consisting merely of a fillet bound round the brow, knotted and falling on the shoulder. He is laid as asleep; his arms crossed upon his body, and his sword by his side. Above him, a bold arched canopy is sustained by two projecting shafts, and on the pinnacle of its roof is the statue of the knight on his warhorse; his helmet, dragon-winged and crested with the dog's head, tossed back behind his shoulders, and the broad and blazoned drapery floating back from his horse's breast,—so truly drawn by the old workman from the life, that it seems to wave in the wind, and the knight's spear to shake, and his marble horse to be evermore quickening its pace, and starting into heavier and hastier charge, as the silver clouds float fast behind it in the sky.

"Now observe, in this tomb as much concession is made to the pride of man as may ever consist with honour, discretion, or dignity. I do not enter into any question respecting the character of Can Grande, though there can be little doubt that he was one of the best among the nobles of his time; but that is not to our purpose. It is not the question whether his wars were just, or his greatness honourably achieved; but whether, supposing them to have been so, these facts are well and gracefully told upon his tomb. And I believe there can be no hesitation in the admission of its perfect feeling and truth. Though beautiful, the tomb is so little conspicuous or intrusive that it serves only to decorate the portal of the little chapel, and is hardly regarded by the traveller as he enters. When it is examined, the history of the acts of the dead is found subdued into dim and minute ornament upon his coffin; and the principal aim of the monument is to direct the thoughts to his image as he lies in death, and to the expression of his hope of resurrection; while, seen as by the memory, far away, diminished in the brightness of the sky, there is set the likeness of his armed youth, stately, as it stood of old in the front of battle, and meet to be thus recorded for us, that we may now be able to remember the dignity of the frame, of which those who once looked upon it hardly remembered that it was dust.

"This, I repeat, is as much as may ever be granted, but this ought always to be granted to the honour and affection of men. The tomb which stands beside that of Can Grande, nearest it in the little field of sleep, already shows the traces of erring ambition. It is the tomb of Mastino II., in whose reign began the decline of his family. It is altogether exquisite as a work of art; and the evidence of a less wise or noble feeling in its design is found only in this, that the image of a virtue, Fortitude, as belonging to the dead, is placed on the extremity of the sarcophagus, opposite to the Crucifixion. But for this slight circumstance, of which the significance will only be appreciated as we examine the series of later monuments, the composition of this monument of Can Mastino would have been as perfect as its decoration is refined. It consists, like that of Can Grande, of the raised sarcophagus, bearing the recumbent statue, protected by a noble four-square canopy, sculptured with ancient scripture history. On one side of the sarcophagus is Christ enthroned, with Can Mastino kneeling before Him; on the other, Christ is represented in the mystical form, half-rising from the tomb, meant, I believe, to be at once typical of His passion and resurrection. The lateral panels are occupied by statues of the saints. At one extremity of the sarcophagus is the Crucifixion; at the other, a noble statue of Fortitude, with a lion's skin thrown over her shoulders, its head forming a shield upon her breast, her flowing hair bound with a narrow fillet, and a three-edged sword in her gauntleted right hand, drawn back sternly behind her thigh, while in her left, she bears high the shield of the Scalas.

"Close to this monument is another, the stateliest and most sumptuous of the three; it first arrests the eye of the stranger, and long detains it—a many pinnacled pile, surrounded by niches with statues of the warrior saints.

"It is beautiful, for it still belongs to the noble time, the latter part of the fourteenth century; but its work is coarser than that of the other, and its pride may well prepare us to learn that it was built for himself, in his own life-time, by the man whose statue crowns it, Can Signorio della Scala. Now observe, for this is infinitely significant. Can Mastino II. was feeble and wicked, and began the ruin of his house;

his sarcophagus is the first which bears upon it the image of a Virtue, but he lays claim only to Fortitude. Can Signorio was twice a fratricide, the last time when he lay upon his death-bed: his tomb bears upon its gables the images of six Virtues—Faith, Hope, Charity, Prudence, and (I believe) Justice and Fortitude."[47]

Not far from "le Arche degli Scaligeri," and going towards the Piazza Indipendenza is a beautiful example of an old house, dating perhaps from the year 1000. Though it is in a dreadful state of neglect and dirt (it is now used for stabling humble vehicles and ponies), the beauty of the brickwork and of different styles of arches—some round, some pointed—is very apparent. The old wooden forked battlements are very uncommon and interesting; and a legend which says that the house was once that of Romeo is so apposite we would fain believe it to be true even while knowing it to be altogether impossible.

CHAPTER IX

Via Cappello—San Fermo—Museo Civico and Picture Gallery

FROM out the active stirring Piazza delle Erbe runs the narrow quiet street of the Via Cappello. The tramway which traverses all Verona from the Porta Nuova to the Porta Vescovo passes at a foot's pace along it, and almost touches an old mediæval house that tradition points out as the house of the Capulets, and where Juliet is said to have lived and loved. A tablet[48] over the door records the legend, though no romance attaches to the use to which the house is now put—a stable for carriers and their vans—and probably few who pass under the archway ever think of the ill-starred lovers or consider their story as aught but a myth.

A little further down the street and on the same side stands the Biblioteca Comunale, where precious volumes and manuscripts are stored in laudable order, and where the kindness and courtesy of the officials makes it a pleasure to study and hunt among the treasures so freely placed at one's disposal. Close beside it is the disused church of St Sebastian; and but a short way further on is the Arco dei Leoni, a Roman ruin, said to have been part of Gallienus's wall, and worthy of a better place and surrounding. A tinsmith's shop is all around it, and zinc baths and tin wares and utensils hang beside the fine columns and architraves that are lost in so incongruous a setting. That this grand old ruin was once one of the gateways into the town seems probable; but archæologists are divided as to its exact origin and purpose, and only agree in claiming for it without hesitation a very remote antiquity. Other houses in this street, now called Via Leoni, have traces of Roman architecture, often stowed away in inner courtyards, and evidently proving of more interest to the passing prying stranger than to the owner and inhabitant.

JULIET'S HOUSE (traditionally)

The church of S. Fermo Maggiore is close at hand; one of the four finest churches of Verona, and beautiful from whichever side we approach it. It is another example of the blending of brick and marble peculiar to Verona; and while studying the harmonious fusion of these materials it is interesting to observe the different periods of building and the different dates that have left their mark on the construction of this noble edifice. The façade, the presbytery, and the belfry are fine examples of the Lombard-Gothic style; and the approach to the principal entrance up a flight of stairs, with tombs, niches, windows around, and a deep portal above is very impressive. To the left of the entrance is the tomb of Aventino Fracastoro, the physician of Cangrande (1350). This monument, of great beauty, consists in true Veronese fashion of the sarcophagus supported on brackets, placed under a canopy. On the other side is another canopy, looking as though intended for a tomb, but of smaller dimensions than the one above-mentioned, and placed there for no reason that has yet been discovered. The actual church of S. Fermo dates from about the year 1065, but the oldest part of it is the crypt which boasts of a very great antiquity. From the archæologist's and historian's point of view the chief interest attaching to S. Fermo centres round this crypt, and they ascribe some portions of it to at least the second half of the eighth century. The different styles of architecture and of fresco-painting in this subterranean church are of all-engrossing matter; and hours might be spent here pondering over the ascendancy of Greek, Roman, Lombard, and Christian art, and deciphering the unmistakable signs that tell how, even in the ninth century, this lower church was decorated with the crude and primitive paintings then coming into vogue. The carvings representing in rude outline the cross in various shape, the fish, and other allegorical symbols point, as far as date is concerned, to a very early period of Christianity, and confirm the generally accepted belief that the crypt was the work of the very first Christians, and built at the moment of the suppression of paganism.

To return however to the church. The interior is striking and beautiful. It consists of a single nave; no aisles are included in the plan, and it is crowned by a magnificent roof made of larch, and shaped like the ribbing of a ship, with paintings and carvings introduced at every possible coign of vantage. The church was first built for the Benedictines in the eleventh century as has been said. Two hundred years later it was transferred to the Franciscans, and it underwent considerable additions and alterations both at their hands, and again in the early part of the fourteenth century. These works were largely helped on by the piety and generosity of Daniele Gusman, the prior of S. Fermo, and by Guglielmo da Castelbarco who, as has been seen, did so much for St Anastasia, and whose tomb standing outside that church has already been described. Here too his memory has been perpetuated in a fresco over the archway to the right and left of the high altar, where he on one side, and Prior Gusman on the other are represented "offering willingly to the Lord." The doubt as to who is the author of these frescoes is still unsolved. For a long time they were attributed to Giotto;

and though Crowe and Cavalcaselle say that none of his work done in S. Fermo is left, they admit that the fresco of Castelbarco presenting the church of S. Fermo is by a different hand to the other frescoes in the church—these latter being all by Veronese masters.

Over the doorway of the main entrance—a door by the way very rarely opened, and to get into the church one must go to the one on the left hand side—is a fresco of the Crucifixion, ascribed first to Cimabue, then to Giotto, and though by neither of them, is at the same time the work of some very early master. To the left of this entrance, and above an ugly mausoleum to the Brenzoni family, is a most beautiful fresco by Vittore Pisanello, and according to Layard, his only fresco-painting, besides the one at St Anastasia, yet remaining in Verona. The subject is the Annunciation, very gracefully and effectively treated, and with some very beautiful architectural drawing around the Madonna. Further on are more frescoes of the fourteenth century, which have not been long discovered, among them being a striking one of the Crucifixion. Close by is the Chapel of the Sacrament, where hangs the masterpiece of Gian Francesco Caroto. It is described as follows by Layard:—"His (Caroto's) best existing work is an altarpiece in the church of S. Fermo Maggiore (Verona), representing the Virgin and Child and St Anne in glory, with four saints beneath, signed and dated 1528. It is grandly conceived, powerful in colour, giving the impression that he had seen and been influenced by Bernardino Luini; the Madonna is a beautiful woman with a tender and gentle expression; the Child less pleasing; the heads of SS. Roch and John are especially fine."[49]

CHURCH OF S. FERMO MAGGIORE
THE MADONNA AND CHILD AND ST ANNE IN
GLORY, WITH OTHER SAINTS BELOW
(G. FRANCESCO CAROTO)

The fresco over a small door leading into the Torriani chapel is by Francesco Bonsignori, signed and dated 1484; and inside the chapel is the tomb raised by Girolamo della Torre, and said to be one of the most precious works of art preserved in S. Fermo. This may doubtless be so for those who first of all are fortunate enough to find some means whereby they can obtain sufficient light to view this treasure; and who secondly are content to be put off with copies of the original. For the bronze bas-reliefs which once decorated this tomb were carried off to Paris, where they are still preserved at the Louvre, and copies supplement the place they once filled. What is left is however pronounced by all who have seen it to be of great merit, and worthy of the designer and artist, Andrea Riccio of Padua.

Several interesting examples of the Veronese school are to be found in this church. In the chapel after that of the Delia Torre family is a good "Adoration" by Orbetto, fine in tone and colour, though the grouping is a little confused and overcrowded. In the chapel dedicated to St Anthony is a picture by Liberale of "St Anthony in Glory," showing, according to Mr Selwyn Brinton, the improvement gained by him after he came "under the influence of the mighty Mantegna, when a greater conception of art seems to strike him."[50] In one of the chapels beside the high altar is a fine Crucifixion by Domenico Brusasorci. The Alighieri chapel is more or less on the lines of the Arco de' Gavi, and was erected by Francesco, the last lineal male descendant of Dante, who with two or three other members of the family, is buried here. The picture over the altar is by Battista del Moro.

A fact that is of botanic interest is to be met with here in the epigraph below the organ to Francesco Calceolari. He was the first botanist who ever made his mark in Verona, and his name at all events suggests some connection with the flower whose gaudy colours were once in such request for the bedding-out garden.

Immediately below the sacristy is the marble sarcophagus erected by the citizens of Verona to the memory of Torello Saraina, who, as has been said, wrote the first printed history of the town, and whose opinion and authority on Veronese antiquities and monuments is of great weight and value. The Saraina chapel standing beside the tomb was erected by the historian himself, and dedicated by him to the Trinity, to the Virgin, and to the Archangel Raphael. It contains a fine painting by Torbido over the altar, a Madonna and Child in the clouds, with the Archangel and Tobias below. According to Morelli, this work makes Torbido worthy to be compared with the elder Bonifazio. The coffin containing the ashes of Saraina was probably removed to the side (where it stands resting on two turrets of marble) when the chapel was arranged for the celebration of the Mass. Saraina died May 8, 1550. That he was a patron of art as well as a man of letters is proved by the fact that not only did he order the fine picture painted by Torbido for the Saraina chapel, but that the house he inhabited in the Via della Stella was also by his desire decorated with frescoes by the same master.

The pulpit is a beautiful bit of fourteenth century work. It is rich in marbles, and has many good designs surmounted with frescoes that for many years were supposed to be the work of Stefano da Zevio. Recent investigations, however, have proved them to be by Martini, whose signature upon them has also come to light.

The patron saint of the church is S. Fermo, who together with S. Rustico, suffered martyrdom early in the fourth century. Their bodies first buried in the crypt were afterwards placed under the high altar in the church, where they were at all events safe from those inundations of the Adige that so often wrought havoc to the town, and that in their impetuosity respected neither saint nor sanctuary. The festival of the martyred saints is held on the 9th of August.

The beautiful exterior of the apse and belfry can be well seen and studied on the way to the Palazzo Pompei. This palace contains the Museo Civico and the Picture Gallery, and stands on the other side of the Adige. The way to it lies across the Ponte delle Navi, a modern bridge built to replace the one set up in 1373 by Cansignorio, which was swept away in the inundation of 1757.

It must seem ungracious on the part of a visitor, and of one too who has received much kindness and courtesy in the town, to complain of the arrangements and methods customary in the public buildings of Verona. But the way in which the works of art are kept and treated is lamentable in the extreme, and the disregard and indifference as to those treasures cannot but evoke feelings of surprise, indignation, and regret. The Palazzo Pompei, a fine Doric building designed by San Micheli, was bequeathed by its late owner to the city for a picture gallery; and that it was never built or intended for the purpose to which it is now put may perhaps serve as some excuse for its total inadequacy. The rooms are small; the windows so placed that a great deal of light falls on some pictures leaving others in darkness, and threatening besides to ruin paintings exposed for hours on bright days to a flood of unmitigated and uncurtained sunshine.

The ground-floor consists of a collection of the most varied kind: there are Etruscan and Roman remains; prehistoric antiquities from the Lake of Garda; marble vases and sculptures, coins, utensils belonging to the prehistoric, bronze, and iron ages; mediæval statues in stone and in bronze; a large array of capitals, columns, and fragments of buildings and fortifications that have been dug up at recent excavations and brought here, and casts of modern works. The great inundation of the Adige in 1882, which is answerable for so much damage in Verona is also held responsible for the state of disorder to which this heterogeneous mass is reduced. The flood disarranged the Museum; and time and money do not yet seem to have been found wherewith to repair the mischief then caused.

The pictures are on the first floor, and are for the most part the works of Veronese masters. The first room, known as the Sala Bernasconi, has a fine but faded picture by Paolo Farinato (No. 13) of Christ shown to the multitude. No. 32 is an early but graceful work by Titian of the Madonna and Child and St John. No. 34, a Madonna and Child, and St John the Baptist with two angels, is said to be by Perugino; and much of it probably is by him, the rest by one of his pupils.

Room II. has several good pictures, though not all are by the artists to whom they are ascribed. No. 86, for instance, is a lovely Presentation in the Temple, with a forged signature of Gian Bellini. No. 88 is a Holy Family by Andrea del Sarto, but so cleaned as to leave little of the original. No. 90 is a Madonna and Child that from its likeness to the fresco in S. Fermo is said to be by Pisanello. No. 92 a Madonna, Francesco Caroto, restored and hard. No. 97, a powerful and authentic portrait by Antonio Moro. No. 120, a Madonna and Child with St Joseph by Perugino. No. 121, a graceful Annunciation by Garofolo. No. 155, a Madonna and Child with two Saints by Francia; a picture full of the charm that this Bolognese master rarely fails to exercise. Nos. 112, 108, and 154, are all by Caroto, though in his earlier rather than in his best and later manner. Other pictures in this room are by good masters but hung so high that all effort to judge of them is vain.

CAVAZZOLA'S DEPOSITION FROM THE CROSS

Room III. has no work in it which demands especial attention.

Room IV., No. 240, a Madonna by Giolfino; a hard and somewhat cold picture though not lacking in expression. No. 243, a Madonna enthroned, with saints and angels; an early work by Paolo Veronese. No. 244, a Madonna and Saints by Antonio Badile; a good picture though hung too high. No. 250, Christ washing the disciples' feet by Bonifazio; a picture full of the rich warm colouring of this master, and lacking—as is often the case with him—in all sense of religious feeling. No. 252, a Madonna enthroned with SS. Roch and Sebastian, by Girolamo dai Libri; and also by him No. 253, the Baptism of Christ. No. 267, a portrait by Paolo Veronese; the only really fine portrait to be found in Verona by Verona's greatest painter, and representing one of the Guarienti family attired as a warrior. No. 271, a Madonna by Bonsignori.

Room V. This is the most interesting room in the gallery. No. 290 is a Holy Family by Girolamo dai Libri, known as "la Vergine dei Conigli," or "of the rabbits." Though somewhat faded and hung too high it is a charming picture representing the Madonna, with St Joseph, St Jerome, and St John the Baptist worshipping the Babe. The landscape is glowing with colour and with rich detail, and the rabbits seated with due solemnity give a humorous touch to the whole scene. There are several important paintings in this room by Paolo Morando surnamed Cavazzola, of whose works in this collection Mr Selwyn Brinton speaks as follows: "In visiting Verona, I found the Public Gallery rich in his paintings; the earnestness of his style, and his power in drawing and colour find illustration in the series of five subjects from the

Passion in that gallery (brought there from S. Bernardino). Most of all among them I gave my admiration to the most striking 'Descent from the Cross,' powerful, of great pathos, brilliant, and yet cold in colour."[51]

Of the power of Cavazzola's painting, and of the decorative value of his work there can be no doubt, but he strikes one as being careful to attain a correct form in his figures rather than to convey depth of devotion, and to be merely affected when he would fain be pathetic. His work at times though very hard and formal is yet often full of expression; his backgrounds are interesting and to be liked; and his vivid colouring is nearly always to be admired. A fine work of his, the last he ever painted, and perhaps his masterpiece, is No. 335 in this room. It is an altarpiece, showing the Madonna in glory with angels, saints, and the donor, the Contessa di Sacco, at the bottom of the picture. Nos. 292, 293, 294, 295 are the series alluded to above; No. 298 is St Thomas questioning our Lord's resurrection by him. Nos. 302 and 303 are also by him; and so too are Nos. 306 and 308. No. 329 is a pleasant portrait by Domenico Brusasorci of himself as a musician. No. 330, the Trinity by Francesco Morone. No. 333, a Madonna and Child with St Andrew and St Peter, by Girolamo dai Libri. No. 334, a very fine Madonna and Child with two saints by Cima da Conegliano. No. 339 is again by Girolamo dai Libri, showing a lovely landscape with an enthroned Madonna, the Child,

St Joseph, Tobias, and the angel all in rich glowing colour, and altogether delightful. There are also three pictures by Caroto in this room: one of the three archangels with Tobias over the door is particularly good. It is signed and is very worthy of notice. On the wall coming into this room is a collection of fragments of miniatures from liturgical books by Liberale, and Girolamo dai Libri. They are all framed, and form as choice and rich a collection of such works of art as exists anywhere.

THE VIRGIN AND CHILD ENTHRONED, WITH ST JOSEPH, THE ARCHANGEL RAPHAEL AND TOBIAS (GIROLAMO DAI LIBRI)

VIRGIN AND CHILD WITH SAINTS IN GLORY (PAOLO MORANDO DETTO CAVAZZOLA)

Room VI. (No. 351), a fine picture of the Madonna and cherubs by Carlo Crivelli showing the influence of the Paduan school. No. 355 is a painting on wood in several compartments by one Turone in a frame of the same date (fourteenth century) and representing divers saints. This picture, dated 1360, is cited by Crowe and Cavalcaselle as a proof of how the Veronese school held aloof from all Giottesque influence. Such independence does not meet with the approval of the two art critics, who refuse to see in this course of action an individuality which declined to borrow even from a superior source—an attitude of originality that was indulged in at a possible loss of increased technique and drawing, but that is worthy all the same of respect.

No. 359 is a painting on wood by Stefano da Zevio: a youthful work, signed and dated 1363, of the Madonna and St Catherine in a garden of roses. No. 362, the Crucifixion by Jacopo Bellini, a grand solemn picture even if somewhat retouched. Nos. 368 and 369 are small altarpieces by Girolamo Benaglio, in frames characteristic of the period (fifteenth century) and in good taste. No. 376, the Resurrection, attributed to Squarcione, and possibly containing some of his work. No. 377, a Deposition by Liberale, but hung too high to be seen well. Nos. 390, 392, 394, are far and away the gems of this room, and are all fine works by Cavazzola. They represent Gethsemane, the Deposition, the Bearing of the Cross. The Deposition is the most famous of this series, which, as shown by the inscription, was painted in 1517, and in it is to be seen the artist's portrait to the left of the cross, while in the background stand out the heights of Verona with the castle of San Pietro and the Adige below.

Few of the other rooms have anything of interest or merit in them, though in No. IX.—when not closed—are to be seen some of the medals of Vittore Pisanello; and a fresco by Cavazzola, brought here from the church of SS. Nazzaro and Celso. There is also a fine fresco in Room XII. by Francesco Morone, of the Madonna with saints, that shows great power of grouping. This was originally on the exterior of a house near the Ponte delle Navi, and was brought here for preservation. Layard says: "A charming specimen of his (Morone's), warm, rich colouring, and delicate and graceful sentiment was, until recently, to be seen in a fresco of the Virgin and Child and saints, on the façade of a house near the Ponte delle Navi at Verona, dated 1515, which added much to the picturesque beauty of the site. It has unfortunately been transferred to canvas, suffering irreparably in the process and by clumsy restoration, and is now a mere wreck in the public gallery."[52]

Here, too, are some frescoes by Martino da Verona, by Giolfino, and by Caroto, and with a glance at them the visit to the picture gallery may be brought to a close.

CHAPTER X

S. Paolo di Campo Marte—SS. Nazzaro e Celso—The Grotto di S. Nazzaro—St Thomas of Canterbury—Giardino Giusti—Sta. Maria in Organo—S. Giovanni in Valle—Teatro Antico—SS. Siro e Libera—Castle of Theodoric—S. Stefano—S. Giorgio in Braida

THE left bank of the Adige lies in that part of the city known as "Veronetta," where several churches are scattered at no wide distances the one from the other; some small and of but meagre interest, others striking both from an historical and artistic point of view. After passing the church of S. Paolo di Campo Marte, where Paolo Farinato lies buried, and where are to be seen works by Girolamo dai Libri, by Paolo Veronese and others; and leaving the little church of S. Giacomo in the Via XX. Settembre, we eventually arrive at the church of SS. Nazzaro e Celso. The external aspect of this church, dating from the eleventh century, is more imposing than the interior which was restored in 1510. Before visiting the church it will be well to go first to the Grotto of S. Nazzaro, a small chapel excavated out of the "tufo," and in which the early Christians met to worship. The walls were evidently once all covered with frescoes, and many traces yet remain which have given rise to much discussion, and about whose date and execution opinions are still divided. Some writers claim for these paintings an epoch as remote as the sixth century, and ascribe them to the period when the Ostrogoths ruled in Verona. Others again say that the very oldest of the paintings are not prior to the year 996, while the latest belong to the eleventh century. There is no doubt whatever that the church or grotto is of far older date than the paintings on the walls; and the historical interest centring around the spot can on no account be called in question. Whatever the date of the frescoes they betoken different periods from their style, the earliest being of a crude, primitive nature that make one at first more inclined to smile than to admire. Those of the second period—among them being our Lord's Baptism in Jordan—have a less comic appearance, while one and all bear traces of the Roman influence which permeated into the works of art carried out by the invaders of Italy in the land of their adoption.

The church of S. Nazzaro consisted originally of five aisles. The restoration brought about in 1510 reduced it to three, and though not as imposing as it must formerly have been, there is a dignified and religious feeling in its present character which suits the traditions that haunt its neighbourhood and hallow to this day the fine Renaissance building. There are many good paintings in the church; in the transept on the right are two panel paintings by

The Story of Verona

Bartolomeo Montagna of St John the Baptist, and of SS. Nazzaro, Celso and Benedict; and in the sacristy there is a Pietà, and a S. Biagio and Sta. Giuliana also by him. (It is impossible not to utter a protest against the state of neglect and decay into which most of the frescoes in this church have fallen, and to hope that some effort may be made to preserve them ere it is too late.) In a beautiful old frame over the altar of S. Biagio is a grand work by Francesco Bonsignori; while in the predella below are some lovely miniatures by Girolamo dai Libri. The dome is decorated with frescoes, all by Falconetto, except the "Annunciation" over the principal door which is by Cavazzola—a fine bit of work. There are more works by this master, as well as others by Brusasorci, Falconetto, Badile, Torbido, and Farinata. Indeed most of the best known Veronese masters have left some evidence of their work in this out-of-the-way church; would that the Veronese of to-day would show themselves worthier of the treasures bequeathed to them by their ancestors, and provide at least for their preservation!

Not far from here after two or three turns to the left rises the church of St Thomas of Canterbury. The doorway is a fine example of Italian Gothic, and some interesting inscriptions beside it relate how the piety of two women of the Stagnolo family contributed towards the work of the façade. Inside the church are some frescoes by Brusasorci; and before the altar of Sta. Maria Maddalena lie the mortal remains of the architect San Micheli, to whom Verona owes so much, and whose work, though so pre-eminently famed for fortified buildings and all relating to military constructions, is admirable in secular and ecclesiastical edifices as well.

Wandering through this part of Verona the eye is often arrested by frescoed palaces and houses of marked architectural beauty and merit, among them being the Casa Barbarani; the Seminario Vescovile; and other houses belonging to private individuals. In the Via Giardino Giusti stands the Palazzo Giusti, a handsome block of masonry, decorated externally by Paolo Farinato, and leading through a pleasant cortile to the beautiful and famous Giardino Giusti. The cypress trees in this part of the garden form its chief glory and renown; and very striking is the view on entering of these grand trees leading up in a straight long avenue to the upper part of the grounds, while single ones dotted about "stand like Druids of old" imparting a sense of solemnity and grandeur to the scene. It is evident that this garden was well known in the seventeenth century from the relation of a Cardinal Rossetti's journey from Cologne to Ferrara via Verona written by his secretary one Vincenzo Armanni. He tells how they embarked at Bussolengo the evening of Friday, July 8, 1644, and came in the space of an hour in a straight course down the Adige to Verona, where they were courteously entertained by the Dominicans. "Saturday the 9th," he writes, "we remained incognito in

Verona, and went to see a most beautiful garden of the Signori Giusti, and many places in that city which in sooth is possessed of conditions so estimable as to cause it to rank among the best in Italy."

WINDOW AND BALCONY IN VIA SEMINARIO

The age of the cypresses is remarkable, some being no less than four hundred, others again five hundred years old;

while only a short time ago a patriarchal giant died at the age of seven hundred years. The lie of the land is also well suited to show off these noble trees to advantage; the ground slopes upwards to the walls of the city till it stops close to where the church of S. Zeno in Monte once stood, and where the tower still stands marking the site of the former monastery. No words can better describe the magnificent view over the town of Verona than those used by Ruskin when he depicts this view, and in language of equal force and beauty presents the panorama, instinct with life and loveliness, to all who have eyes to see and to read. He wrote, it is true, from another spot, but he might have been standing on the upper terrace of the Giardino Giusti when he penned the following lines so admirably does the description tally with the scene here laid before us.

The Story of Verona

GIARDINO GIUSTI

"There is, first, this blue Lombardic plain, wide as the sea, and in the very centre of it, at about twelve miles away from you, a little cluster of domes and towers, with a gleam of white water round them. That is Mantua. Look beyond its fretted outline, and you will see that in that direction the plain, elsewhere boundless, is ended by undulations of soft hills. Those are the Apennines above Padua. Then look to the left, and just beyond the roots of the Alps, you will see the cluster of the cones of the Euganean hills, at the space at their feet in which rests Padua, and the gleam of the horizon beyond them in which rests Venice. Look then, north-eastward, and touched into a crown of strange rubies as the sun descends, there is the snowy cluster of the Alps of Friuli. Then turn to the north-west, and under the sunset itself you will see the Adige flow from its enchanted porch of marble, and in one strong and almost straight stream, blanched always bright by its swiftness, reflecting on its eddies neither bank nor cloud, but only light, stretch itself along the vines, to the Verona lying at your feet; there first it passes the garden wall of the church of S. Zeno, then under the battlements of the great bridge of the Scaligers, then passes away out of sight behind the hill on which, though among ghastly modern buildings, here and there you may still trace a grey fragment of tower and wall—the remnants of the palace of Theodoric of Verona—Dietrich of Bern.

"Now I do not think that there is any other rock in all the world, from which the places and monuments of so complex and deep a fragment of the history of its ages can be visible, as from this piece of crag, with its blue and prickly weeds. For you have thus beneath you at once, the birthplaces of Virgil and of Livy; the homes of Dante and Petrarch; and the source of the most sweet and pathetic inspiration of your own Shakespeare; the spot where the civilization

The Story of Verona

of the Gothic kingdoms was founded on the throne of Theodoric, and where whatever was strongest in the Italian race redeemed itself into life by its league against Barbarossa. You have the cradle of natural science and medicine in the schools of Padua; the central light of Italian chivalry in the power of the Scaligers; the chief stain of Italian cruelty in that of Ezzelin; and, lastly, the birthplace of the highest art; for among these hills, or by this very Adige bank, were born Mantegna, Titian, Coreggio, and Veronese."[53]

Beyond the Garden Street of the Giusti lies the tract of the "Acqua Morte," formed by the branch or canal of the Adige, which once flowed here but was filled in in 1895 when the great works of the "muraglioni" were executed which have confined the river into bounds which it cannot pass, nor break the limits now imposed upon it. In this quarter is the church of Sta. Maria in Organo, another of the Veronese churches of special interest and individuality. The date of the church is uncertain, but of its antiquity there can be no doubt, some writers placing it even as far back as the sixth century. The foundation of the monastery of Sta. Maria in Organo is ascribed to the piety of the Lombard Duke Lupone and his wife Ermelinda in the year A.D. 615. The actual building was erected on the site of an older one in 1131. It was committed to the monks of Monte Oliveto in 1444; shortly after that date the campanile was added, and San Micheli began the façade which for some unknown reason was never completed. The interior of the church is rich in paintings and frescoes, every chapel having its picture over the altar, and the sides being decorated as well. There are some fine frescoes in the nave from Old Testament scenes, which are probably by Brusasorci, though occasionally ascribed to Francesco Morone. A great deal of Morone's work is to be found here both in the church and sacristy, and speaking of this latter Layard says: "He (Morone) excelled as a painter in fresco, as he has shewn in the decoration of the sacristy of the church of Sta. Maria in Organo in Verona, in which he has introduced half-length figures of popes, monks, and nuns, of the Olivetan order."[54]

THE GIUSTI GARDEN

Over the third altar on the left facing the high altar is "the most lovely Madonna and Child under a canopy adorned with flowers; on each side an angel sings and plays. Below, the stately figures of SS. Augustine and Martin. A very fascinating work. Signed work (1503), painted apparently on silk backed by canvas."[55] The detail of this picture is exquisite; the composition powerful, and the grace and dignity of each figure in turn is striking. There are fine paintings throughout the church all by Veronese masters, the most marked among them being by Brusasorci, Giolfino, Farinato, Caroto, Balestra, Zavoldo, Torbido. The chapel in the right transept contains a Sta. Francesca Romano by Guercino, with paintings on the side by Cavazzola. In the chapel to the left of the choir is a picture of St Benedict by Brentana. This picture serves as a screen, and is sometimes removed when a quaint mediæval statue is revealed of our Lord seated on the ass's colt. The statue, of a great age, is known as "La Muletta," and is an object of great veneration. It is shown to the public on Palm Sunday when no doubt the gaudy colours—for the figure and animal though of wood are painted—impress each gazer's eye with wonder and admiration. Above the seats of the high altar are frescoed landscapes by Cavazzola and Brusasorci.

The centre of interest in this church culminates however in the sacristy which Vasari rightly pronounced to be one of the most beautiful in Italy. On the right hand side are some lovely intarsia panels by Fra Giovanni da Verona, one of the monks belonging to the monastery of this church. "The rich play of fancy shown by this illustrious brother deserves a volume and a pen of gold to describe it," says an Italian writer; "festoons of fruit and flowers, sphinxes, chimeras, birds, perspective—all is wrought with a perfect and exquisite sense of art, all has succeeded in producing an unparalleled harmony of line and colour in a calm outpouring of inspiration, in a continuous and marvellous freshness."[56] The richness of design employed is indeed wonderful, and is only equalled by the execution of the work. The carving is as perfect and delicate as it is bold and crisp; and it is not difficult to believe that this intarsia possesses the renown of being the most perfect of its kind in Italy. Above these lovely panels are frescoes by Morone of the Olivetan monks in their white garbs; while again in the lunettes overhead are portraits of the popes who were elected out of the order to fill the Papal See. In a corner by the door leading into the choir and almost concealed by a cupboard is the portrait of Fra Giovanni himself, the friar who as has been said did this intarsia work, the greatest master of the kind that Italy has ever produced. He died in 1520. The frescoes are all by Morone, and it has well been said that this sacristy is a masterpiece of Veronese art. There is also here a lovely picture by Girolamo dai Libri, the "Madonna del Limone," of the Blessed Virgin enthroned, with St Stephen and St Catherine below, a delightful setting of leaves, fruit, and architectural detail, all in a flood of sunlight which enhances the effect a hundredfold.[57]

DOORWAY OF CARVED WOOD IN THE
SACRISTY OF S. MARIA

The choir of the monks opens out from the sacristy, and here again are treasures of carving and of inlaid woodwork also by Fra Giovanni, possessing a topographical value as well as an artistic one in that they represent views of the city of that date and place before us scenes which no longer exist. There are here views of Rome also; and the value of such abiding testimony as to "the days that are no more," is enough in itself to make one linger in the church of Sta.

Maria in Organo, and muse in delight and wonder over the industry and talent that prompted this labour of love so many centuries ago. In the choir there is also a magnificent candelabrum equally by Fra Giovanni, carved in walnut wood; and the carving and inlay work testify anew to the craft and power of this frate, and prove him to have been indeed a consummate master of his art. The inundation of 1882 did frightful damage to the woodwork in this church; and though the damage has been remedied to a great extent traces of it yet remain and show to what an extreme peril these treasures were exposed.

Beyond the church of Sta. Maria in Organo the winding narrow by-way of S. Giovanni in Valle leads to the little church of the same name. Its antiquity is great seeing that it dates from the fifth century; and its plan of erection, its crypt, and all its accessories point to its being one of the earliest churches in Verona. There are frescoes by Brusasorci, and Giolfino, inside, and traces of paintings of a far earlier date than these are being discovered under the whitewash and plaster that cover the walls. Fragments of Roman remains are to be found near the tower and the cloisters, and here too is the peculiar sort of column similar to the one in the Piazza delle Erbe and in the Piazza Brà, and which gives evidence that a market-place once stood there. In the beautiful crypt are two sarcophagi of Greek marble, dating from the very earliest days of Christianity. One of them is supposed to contain the bones of St Simon and St Jude; and both of them have bas-reliefs of great interest and originality. The fresco over the principal entrance is by Stefano da Zevio, and close beside are two modern windows that sadly deface the pure early style of the façade.

The next point of interest that we come to is the "Teatro Antico," the old theatre of the Romans, which is said to have been built in the age of Augustus. In true Roman fashion it is posted on the side of a hill; this plan for saving labour together with increased convenience in the construction of a theatre being often resorted to in days of old. Nor was the hill at the back the only natural adjunct to the theatre. The river was also turned on to aid in whatever scenery required water effects, and above all for the naval displays that formed a part in the representations which were given in the theatre. The excavations made here in 1836 by Cav. Andrea Monga have brought to light almost all that remains of this ruin, and revealed what has so far escaped the destroying hand of Time. There is not however a great deal to be seen, for one thing after another has combined to wreck this archæological relic. An earthquake in the year 793 damaged it to a great extent; and rather more than a century later tradition says that Berengarius I., under the impression that its stability was of so insecure a nature as to threaten every habitation in its neighbourhood, issued a decree that anyone who chose might demolish it and carry away the materials to use as they saw fit. How many a building in Verona may not have been enriched with stones, or capitals, or columns from this mighty ruin! It is interesting to see among the recent excavations some of the seats where the spectators once sat in rows, together with what is said to have been the box with the name over its entrance of a private family, and part of the stage, and to wander among the ruins of what must certainly have been one of the finest theatres of antiquity.

CHOIR STALL OF INTARSIO WORK IN S. MARIA

At no distance from the "Teatro Antico" rises the little church of SS. Siro and Libera, built over a part of the theatre, and deriving a legendary interest from the tradition that Christianity was introduced into Verona by S. Siro, and that the first time mass was ever celebrated in the town it was celebrated by the saint in the church now dedicated to him and to Sta. Libera.

The ground around and about here is replete with associations of Roman and Gothic times, and with the very earliest existence of Verona as a town; for the hills above this left bank of the Adige—the hills of S. Pietro and S. Felice—are the sites where the first inhabitants of the city had their dwelling. On the "colle di S. Pietro" stood the castle of Theodoric, King of the Ostrogoths, of whom Carlo Cipolla (the most trustworthy of Verona's modern historians) says: "He embellished Verona with baths, with palaces, with covered ways; he fortified it with new walls, and renewed the aqueduct thereof. Considerable traces of his palace on St Peter's hill still remain in the walls which encircle the summit, and which are built on the Roman system.... Less numerous and less evident are the vestiges of his real and own palace which stood on the part of the hill overlooking the river, and it is not always easy to distinguish between what actually belonged to the palace of Theodoric and what were fragments appertaining to the theatre that stood below." On a previous page speaking of Theodoric the same writer says: "In the poetic legends of Germany the king is called Theodoric of Verona, Dietrich von Bern! The last chapters of the *Nibelungenlied* are filled with tales of his heroic deeds and with those of his warriors. Likewise in Germany up to the time of Frederick II. of Swabia, and maybe even after Verona was known as 'Dietrich's Bern.' The mountaineers of Giazza to this day never speak of Verona save as 'Bearn,' which is nothing after all but the Latin name turned into German."[58]

The king of the Ostrogoths, as has been said, spent his time gladly in Verona; but little remains of his buildings or fortifications, imposing as they must have been. The walls he set up have been built over by Cangrande, who erected those with forked battlements which remain to this day, a token of picturesque strength to the town, stamping it for ever as a city whose bulwarks can defy every foe, and laugh to scorn every invader.

The Castel di S. Pietro is now a fortress, so too is the Castel di S. Felice, which stands on the hill above it; and from both these forts magnificent views can be had over the city.

Beyond the Ponte di Pietra, and almost at the very bend of the river, stands the church of S. Stefano, for many years the Cathedral of Verona, and linked with all its early history, and with days of persecution and trouble. This church, standing on the foundations of a former one destroyed by

King Theodoric, was rebuilt in the eleventh century, though the crypt and choir are of an earlier period, and are both beautiful and interesting in the character and originality of their conception.

CHURCH OF S. GIORGIO IN BRAIDA, MARTYRDOM OF ST GEORGE (PAOLO VERONESE)

The whole plan—though on far smaller and simpler lines—recalls that of S. Zeno, for here again is the nave and two side aisles, as well as the three floors formed by the crypt, the central building, and the raised choir. This latter forms a striking feature in S. Stefano; and very remarkable indeed it is with its rough-hewn bishop's throne—recalling the one in the cathedral church of Torcello, erected there in 1008—and leading to another and older choir beyond, both of which are decorated with frescoes. From the older choir a passage communicates with the crypt, a most unusual contrivance, and one that serves perhaps to demonstrate that those parts of the building date from the same epoch. The crypt is in the form of a Latin cross, and has rows of columns disposed somewhat in the same fashion as those in the crypt of S. Fermo, save that at S. Stefano the columns are of Oriental marble. Many of the bishops of Verona lie buried in this crypt, together with forty martyrs who were done to death in the reign of Diocletian. Here too is the tomb of Galla Placidia, the daughter of the Emperor Valentinian, and wife of Olibrius, Emperor of the East. An ancient statue of St Peter stands in the church, and there are besides several paintings by Brusasorci, Farinato, Giolfino, and other Veronese painters. The façade of the church is impressive, dating probably from the eleventh century, though a careful study will detect traces of a still earlier date; and were it possible to remove two or three additions made in more recent times, the original frontage would stand out in all its simplicity and beauty.

A little further on is the church of S. Giorgio in Braida, or S. Giorgio Maggiore, as it is also called, a building partly raised by San Micheli. This church contains some very fine pictures, for the most part by Veronese masters. Behind the high altar is a grand painting by Paolo Veronese, of peculiar value, as few of his works are to be met with in his native town, most of them having found a home in Venice, the scene of his labours, and where he lived and worked and died. The subject is the martyrdom of St George; and apart from the fine treatment of the figures, the boldness of outline and depth of colour, the picture is intensely interesting as showing the artist's own portrait in the person of the warrior on horseback in the left hand corner. On either side of this picture are two good paintings, the one on the right by Felice Brusasorci, of the giving of the manna in the desert, fine in tone and in conception, though finished by his pupils; the other by Paolo Farinato in extreme old age, when perhaps his hand had lost some of its cunning. Farinato's portrait is to be seen in a group of his own family painted in a corner of the picture. The altar below the organ, the first on the right coming down the church, contains a beautiful work by Alessandro Bonvicini of Brescia, known as "Il Moretto," of St Cecilia between St Catherine, St Lucy, and other saints, with the Virgin above. This picture bears the inscription, "Alexandro Morettus Brix. MDXC." Just beyond is a most lovely Virgin and Child by Girolamo dai Libri, also signed by the author, and dated 1526. The Virgin, who is enthroned, has S. Lorenzo Giustinian on her right, and S. Zeno on her left; below are three exquisite angels, two of whom are singing, while the third accompanies them on the lute. The detail of the picture is of the same lovely and finished order in which this great miniaturist delighted and excelled, and which he introduced into almost all his work. The third altar has paintings, by Caroto, of SS. Roch and Sebastian; and by Domenico Brusasorci, of the Apostles exorcising an evil spirit. Beyond that is the martyrdom of Lorenzo by Sigismondo da Stefano; and a not very beautiful St Ursula is in the adjoining chapel by Caroto. In the second altar coming down the church on the left are some angels by Brusasorci; and an Annunciation by Caroto, in which the Archangel Gabriel is more beautiful to look on than the Blessed Virgin. Above the main door is a picture of our Lord's Baptism by Tintoretto, but hung at so great a height it is not easy to see.

THE MADONNA WITH HOLY WOMEN
(MORETTO DU BRESCIA)

The way back into the town leads either across the modern iron bridge called after Garibaldi, or by that known as the Ponte della Pietra, a magnificent example of Roman work, and one of the most picturesque bridges in Verona. The two arches towards the hill are of recognised Roman construction; the rest leading into the town and towards the tower on that side erected by the Scaligers, is said to be the work of Fra Giocondo in 1521. Soon after crossing the "Pons marmoreus," as it was also called, we come to an old house at the bend of the road and facing the bridge which has a fresco painted under the eaves depicting the wares sold in the shop below, among which may be seen a bunch of tallow candles tied by their wicks and suspended on high—a practice familiar enough among ourselves. The painting was done in the "cinque cento," and the trade of "wholesale grocer" goes on in the building to-day as it did some five centuries ago.

In the Via Cappelletta, that opens out from the Via Ponte Pietra, is a house which claims to have been that of the Capulets—a claim that has no foundation, and that perhaps has only been raised in order to entice the passer-by to go in to see a very pretty courtyard, which certainly deserves a moment's glance if the inspection of the many sights of "Veronetta" has not exhausted all our powers of endurance.

CHAPTER XI

Sant' Eufemia—Porta dei Borsari—S.S. Apostoli—S. Lorenzo—S. Bernardino—Sta. Trinità—Tomb of Romeo and Juliet—Ponte Rofiolo—Piazza Brà

The church of Sant' Eufemia may be reached either by following the broad open way of the Lungadige Panvinio, or by proceeding along the Corso Porta Borsari and turning up to the right. The church, of Gothic style, dates from the thirteenth century, but it is much spoilt internally by modern restorations. The façade is imposing, and each side of the door is flanked by a tomb: that on the right being a grand sarcophagus of the fourteenth century of red Verona marble to the Cavalcani-Bandi family; the one on the left, of the sixteenth century, by San Micheli, to the Counts Lavagnolo. There is also some more of San Micheli's work to be seen close to a lateral door on the south side in the shape of a monument to the Verită family; while over this same door is a fresco by Stefano da Zevio. San Micheli was also the designer for the cloister of this church. Inside, the building strikes one as cold and poor. There are though some good frescoes by Caroto and Domenico Brusasorci, and an altar-piece by this latter of the Madonna in glory may certainly rank among his best works. In the Spolverini Chapel (to the proper left of the high altar) are some very interesting frescoes by Caroto "representing the story of Tobias, in which the compositions are skilfully balanced, the personages natural in movement and expression, and the colouring especially entitled to commendation."[59]

BALCONY IN VIA S. EUFEMIA

Returning to the Corso di Porta Borsari the ancient church of S. Giovanni in Foro (so called because it was close to the old Roman Forum) stands to the right, and claims a moment's attention on account of its Gothic wall decorations, and the fresco by Domenico Brusasorci of the "Deposition from the Cross." There is also here an inscription let into the wall which tells that in the year A.D. 1172 a fire devastated the town of Verona. Beyond the little church rises the Porta dei Borsari, the famous Roman gateway, or, it may be, triumphal arch. It consists of a double archway with two storeys of windows overhead, while the side looking towards the Corso Cavour retains still the carvings and ornamentations round the architraves and on the sides. The style is Corinthian, having pediments over the archways as well as over the windows on the upper storeys, while spiral fluted columns flanking these windows bring in a style of architecture of a different character and form an anomaly altogether unexpected. Opinions differ as to the date of this archway, some placing it at the year A.D. 265 when Roman art was at a low ebb, others maintaining that it shows evidence of a good period as to style, and that an inscription which it bore in honour of the Emperor Gallienus was not of the same date as the archway. This inscription was formed of bronze letters fastened in relief upon the stone. These letters were removed at a very early date, but the marks they left served for deciphering the words originally placed on

The Story of Verona

the archway. The conclusion generally arrived at as to the age of the building is that it was probably erected at the time of Vespasian, or of the Antonines—a good period as far as the art of building was concerned—and that in spite of its inconsistencies it is a remarkable and grand piece of architecture, forming a link of consummate interest between the Verona of to-day and the great Roman Empire of more than fifteen hundred years ago.

Immediately beyond the "Porta" the street opens out into the Corso Cavour, and some interesting houses and palaces spring up around. There is first the house of the painter Nicolò Giolfino, where some restored and damaged frescoes are all that is left of the decoration once lavished on this house by Andrea Mantegna. Opposite in the little square of S. Micheletto stands a column surmounted by a lamb, placed there to mark that at one time the Guild of Wool—"Arte della Lana"—whose device was a lamb bearing a banner, had their offices there. Immediately beside the column stands the Palazzo Carlotti, a handsome though somewhat heavy edifice of the decadent period, with an ornate door set in a colonnade. This is followed by the Casa Pozzoni, a palace of Venetian Gothic of the fourteenth century, fine and well preserved. Facing it is a still finer building, the Palazzo della Banca Nazionale, with beautiful balconies, windows, and decorations, all good specimens of the best Renaissance date. Further on is the Piazza dei

S.S. Apostoli, where a statue to the poet and patriot Aleardi (born in Verona in 1812) was put up in 1878, the very year in which he died. The sculptor was Ugo Zannini, the same who executed the statue to Dante in the Piazza dei Signori. Behind Aleardi's statue is the church of the S.S. Apostoli, with that of Sta. Fosca and Sta. Teuteria annexed to it. These churches date from very early times, that of the S.S. Apostoli being prior to the eleventh century, and they bear to this day traces of the construction carried out at so remote an epoch. The apse and the belfry are Romanesque; and at the side of the belfry are some primitive stone sarcophagi that belonged of old to three patrician families of Verona. The interior of the church contains some fine Lombard-Byzantine decorations, and some later ones of the Renaissance epoch. The Virgin Saints Sta. Fosca and Sta. Teuteria—(and might one without undue levity or irreverence venture to inquire if this latter were the patron saint of toy terriers?) lie buried in the little church that bears their names. This church is of even earlier date than that of the S.S. Apostoli, being said to belong to the eighth century, and to have been consecrated in 751. There are tombs within it of the Bevilacqua family, whose palace close by was designed by San Micheli, and is looked upon as one of his masterpieces.

CORSO CAVOUR

Opposite Aleardi's statue and on the other side of the Corso Cavour is the church of S. Lorenzo, which stands off from the street, and is reached under an archway, which bears a figure of the saint aloft holding his gridiron, and through a picturesque courtyard. It is said that this church is built on the ruins of a Roman basilica dedicated presumably to Venus, and that it dates from the fifth century. The plan is altogether on the lines of the Roman basilicas, and consists of two tiers, the upper one having been set apart for the use of the women. This again was split up into compartments, one being for the virgins, another for the widows, and another for the matrons. The style of this church is Roman-Lombardesque, and in spite of a good deal of misdirected zeal and modern renovation there is much to admire in the building. The plans for restoring it to its original condition are also to be admired and encouraged, and one can but wish success to Don Pietro Scapini, the worthy vicar of the church, for his schemes for lowering the floor to its former level, and for other designs calculated to add to the beauty and interest of the old church of S. Lorenzo. The round towers at the west front are striking and characteristic. They led up formerly to the women's gallery, and have curious circular basements, not often to be seen, though similar ones exist in one or two other places in Verona. The round arches in the interior of S. Lorenzo are very fine; and the alternate columns and pillars are of Veronese and foreign marbles and have all differently ornamented capitals. The material of which the church is chiefly built—"tufo" and brick—is very effective, and the layers of alternate red and yellow form a mixture of colour at once harmonious and peculiar. The discovery of frescoes on the walls points strongly to the probability that once the church was all covered with paintings; many doubtless having still to come to light, while others have disappeared irretrievably. Above the high altar is a Madonna and Child in the clouds by Domenico Brusasorci, with S.S. John and Lorenzo below (1566).

Emerging again into the Corso Cavour, and on this same right hand side, is the Palazzo Portalupi, with an Ionic front of the eighteenth century, but "barocco" as to style, and over-ornamented. A little higher up—always on the same side—is the Palazzo Canossa, by San Micheli, one of the finest palaces in this Corso, and commanding an extensive view over the Adige and the country beyond it. The next point of interest is the Castel Vecchio, built as we have seen by Cangrande II. between the years 1353 and 1358. It will also be remembered that this second Cangrande della Scala built too the bridge across the river opening out from the castle, whereby he could receive help from Germany, and over which it may be that the hosts of Brandenburg marched to his assistance into the city. A third arch was added to the bridge in later times in order to strengthen it against the impetuous rush of the Adige; and the whole surmounted with the forked battlements wherewith the Scaligers usually crowned their buildings is a marked addition to the beauty of this mediæval stronghold. It is now used as a barrack, but carts and wagons cross under the archway over the bridge, and foot passengers may go in and out as their business or fancy leads them. It is well to stand for a while on the bridge to ponder over the days of yore and to watch the rapid, swirling river as it rushes along, oblivious of Past and Present, and seeking only in headlong fashion to reach the home which awaits it in the far off distant sea.

From the Castel Vecchio the "Stradone di S. Bernardino" leads away to the left till it reaches the church of that name. The entrance into the church is through a cloister, to which some courteous monks open the door, and show the way into the building itself. This is of the fifteenth century, and belongs to the Franciscan brotherhood. The rood screen and organ loft are worthy of notice, but the object of special interest is the beautiful "Cappella Pellegrini," a gem in its way, and the masterpiece—in so far as a religious edifice is concerned—of San Micheli. It is a circular chapel in Renaissance style, and was erected by Margherita Pellegrini to the memory of her husband. The decorations and classical severity of the pediments, cornices, and pilasters are considered almost faultless as to symmetry and design. The fact that San Micheli did not superintend its completion may account however for some blemishes, and for the falling away from the absolute purity of style which would otherwise have doubtless been preserved. In spite of this it is an exquisite piece of graceful refined work, unique in its way, and an abiding proof of the versatility and power of Verona's greatest architect. It must be owned that there is no picture of extraordinary renown in this church, those that possessed any special merit having been transferred to the Public Gallery, and copies placed in their stead. There is however a good Crucifixion, by Francesco Morone in the interesting Cappella di Sta. Croce, and other fair work by Nicolò Giolfino and Caroto. To the left of the altar is a good picture by Benaglio of the Madonna and saints, "inscribed with his name, with an architectural background and festoons of fruit and flowers, such as painters of the (Veronese) school were fond of introducing into their pictures."[60] The pictures in S. Bernardino are for the most part by the less famous of the Veronese masters, and the celebrity of the church rests mainly on the classical architectural merits of the Pelligrini Chapel. The cloisters are lined with tablets and mortuary records, for the cemetery of the town existed for some twenty years here before it was transferred, nearly a century ago, to the site which it now occupies on the other side of the Adige just below the iron bridge, the Ponte Aleardi.

*FRESCO BY DOMENICO MORONE
IN THE LIBRARY OF S. BERNARDINO*

The Library of S. Bernardino (now a boys' school) contains a striking fresco by Domenico Morone, which is rarely seen by the traveller though well worth a visit on account of its individuality and interest. The fresco—a large composition divided into three parts by classical columns, represents Franciscan saints and dignitaries. In the centre is placed the Madonna and Child enthroned, with numerous saints around them, among them being the donors of the painting under the form of St Francis and Sta. Chiara. The effect of the background, giving as it does the idea of a distant and most lovely landscape, is beautiful, and goes far to redeem the stiffness of outline evident in the drawing and the awkward treatment of the figures and drapery.

Following the road which runs beside the grand wall of bastions set up by the Viscontis, we gain a small height on which stands the church of Sta. Trinità. On the right going up the slope is the former church of Sta. Maria degli Angeli, now used as a college for girls of good families, but containing no treasures of art. The little hill is known as the "clivo del Monte Oliveto" from the Olivetan monks who came from Vallombrosa to settle here, and to build the church of Sta. Trinità, which was consecrated in 1117. The façade of the church is lovely, with beautiful arches severe in their simplicity, and in the grace and evenness of their design. In fact simplicity is the keynote of the front and vestibule of this church, and in spite of the alterations and restorations now going on, this characteristic has been successfully maintained. The building is in sad need of funds, and it is easy to see how beautiful the church could again become once many an arch, now filled in, were opened out, and the original scheme adhered to and executed. This scheme was symbolical as well as beautiful, for not only is it clear that the steps which led down into the church were meant to be so to show that man should humble himself when about to enter the house of God, but also the right transept (the church is cruciform) has a curved irregular shape, intended to represent the pressure made on the cross by our Lord's right shoulder weighing more heavily on that side of it. There are some fine frescoes above the principal arch that have only just been uncovered, but their authorship is unknown. The exterior of the east end of the church is very interesting and well worth inspecting. To arrive there one must go through a side corridor and the sacristy, and then one comes upon as fine an apse and belfry as can well be seen. Here is some remarkable Roman masonry with the oft-repeated layers of "tufo," and brick, together with dentellated work, now in brick and now in stone, which is very effective and shows off forcibly some carved heads placed immediately under a succession of arches. Two shapeless and ugly windows have been opened out on both sides of the apse, and wanton sacrilegious hands have ruthlessly broken through a large portion of the beautiful work of Roman days. The belfry too is a grand specimen of Roman building, combining the force and beauty of vigour and stability with all the grace and loveliness of proportion and elegance; and this out-of-the-way unknown bell-tower may certainly rank as one of the loveliest among the many lovely ones here in Verona.

Below the church of Sta. Trinità and now leading past a huge barrack built by the Austrians, runs the old Roman road which led out towards Ostiglia on the Po, and into the town through the gate formerly known as that of Sta. Croce. It was along this road that the race was run to which Dante alludes in the *Inferno*—

... "e parve di coloro
Che corrono a Verona il drappo verde
Per la campagna; e parve di costoro
Quegli che vince e non colui che perde."[61]
—(*Inf.* xv. 121, etc.)

Mr Vernon says:[62] "During his sojourn at Verona Dante would often have witnessed the foot race that took place annually on the first Sunday in Lent for the *Pallio*, or green mantle, in which race Boccaccio says the runners were naked.... Scartazzini says this popular spectacle was instituted to celebrate the victory that was won on the 29th September 1207, by Azzo d'Este, Podestà of Verona, over the adherents of the Conte di San Bonifazio and the Conte Montecchi. The statutes of Verona state that four prizes were to be exhibited for competition, the first of which was to be run for by virtuous women, even if *only one* could be found."

Soon after the Palazzo Gazzalo, which boasted a fine garden now only kept as a nursery garden, is the old church of the Cappucines, with traces here and there of Roman masonry. It is now given up to the manufacture of torpedo boats. A few paces further on (going always towards the town) we come to a large enclosure where a horse fair is held twice a year, and where a brisk trade is done in that line, horses to the number of about a thousand coming from Italy, Hungary and other countries to be bought and sold. Through this modern commercial part of Verona we pass to the garden of the Orfanotrofio, where the made-up tomb of Romeo and Juliet has been placed. The tomb is of red Verona marble, but before it was put to this use it served as a washing-trough. A feeling of pity and disdain cannot but be felt over the fraud here practised to arouse false sentimentality. The story of the two lovers, as is well known, had no foundation, and was taken by Shakespeare from one of the tales of Luigi di Porto, a novelist of the sixteenth century. The enmity between the two houses of Montagu and Capulet was indeed a fact historically true, and a fact also whose effect made itself felt in the civil wars and dissensions that had so often disturbed the internal life of Verona. This enmity has also been noticed by Dante, who speaks of it in the *Purg*. vi. 107. But the very silence maintained by the great Tuscan over the story of the lovers is proof enough that so touching a romance had no foundation. Had there been one we may be sure that the master-hand at whose touch Paolo and Francesca have been endowed with immortal fame, and who in six short lines has sketched for us the tragedy of *La Pia*, would not have left "unwept, unhonoured and unsung" the memory of the lovers of Verona. Romeo and Juliet lived only in the imagination of our great dramatist, who has bestowed on them a fame and immortality which they could never have gained for themselves, and which has endeared them to every heart.

The Story of Verona

The bridge called "Rofiolo" leads into the wide Via Pallone, and close beside it is to be seen a tablet with some heads carved on it in high relief. The story of this tablet and of the strange name of "Rofiolo" has been explained as follows: some "guilty sons" (*rei figli*, hence *rofiolo*) murdered their parents and threw them into the canal which flows hard by. The name of these "guilty sons" has consequently been affixed to the spot where their iniquity was perpetrated, and their effigies have been placed near at hand. Such at least is the tradition, into whose absolute veracity it were perhaps well not to inquire too closely.

The Via Pallone leads into the Piazza Vittorio Emanuele, or Piazza Brà (from Preatum, a meadow) where on one side is an equestrian statue of Victor Emanuel by Borghi, placed there in 1883. The Arena on the east side of the Square forms naturally enough the chief object of interest, but there are also some buildings and palaces around for which a moment's notice may be claimed. The double archway which leads out of the Piazza into the Corso Vittorio Emanuele dates from the epoch of the Scaligers, or more probably from that of the Visconti, as does also the pentagonal tower beside it. Close to this again is the Palazzo della Gran Guardia Vecchia, a huge massive building ascribed to one Curtoni (1609), a pupil of San Micheli. It was built for public meetings, concerts, lectures and the like, and serves for such purposes still. On the other side of the archway, or as it is called, the Portone della Brà, is the Museo Lapidario, which stands inside the courtyard of the Philharmonic Theatre. It was founded and organised by the historian Scipione Maffei, and contains a large amount of precious lapidary relics among which are to be discovered runic, Latin, Greek, Arabic, Egyptian, Persian and Hebrew inscriptions. The most fashionable cafés are also to be found in this Piazza, and in hot weather those inhabitants of Verona who cannot escape for change of air and scene to the country wend their way thither to court the fresh breeze of the wide open square at even-time.

CHAPTER XII

San Zeno

THE road to S. Zeno leads straight past the Castel Vecchio; and away from the noise and bustle of the town we approach one of the finest examples of a Romanesque church to be found in the whole of Northern Italy. A quiet dignity and simplicity may be said to be the characteristics of this glorious basilica both within and without; while the blending of pagan antiquity and Christian feeling has brought about a harmony in expression and construction that is very impressive. Tradition has it that King Pepin, Charlemagne's son, was the founder, but no document exists to prove this, though the belief that it was begun about the year 900, and that its erection was gone on with for two succeeding centuries, has much to support it. It is certain that the Emperor Otho I. of Germany on his way to Rome through Verona sojourned for a while at the monastery of S. Zeno, and left a large sum of money with the Bishop Rathold towards the fund for the completion of the church. There is not a corner of S. Zeno that is not of interest, and this begins with the west front, with the portals, and with the doors, each one claiming in turn its meed of praise and admiration. The church has been enlarged and restored, but nevertheless it retains its noble proportions intact, and modern works have done little to injure the plan and construction of the building. The façade is embellished with bas-reliefs, carved in the yellow stone of the country, and taken from legendary and sacred subjects. In the right hand corner the legend of King Theodoric is represented, for it is supposed that he is the warrior here at the chase, pursuing the stag which cannot be caught, and in whose pursuit the hunter rides on till he reaches the gates of hell. The sculptures are rough and uncouth, but full of life and movement, and were executed in the year 1139 by Wiligelmus and Nicolaus, this latter being the same artist whose work has already been noticed at the Duomo. The round window above the portal stands for the wheel of fortune, with figures in different attitudes to express the moods of the changeable goddess. On the outer circle is engraved in leonine lines:—

"En ego Fortuna moderor mortalibus una,
Elevo, depono, bona cunctis vel mala dono."

which may be loosely rendered—

"Behold, I, Fortune, I alone bestow on mortals,
I raise, depose; to all I give or good or evil gifts."

On the inner circle is written:—

"Induo nudatos, denudo veste paratos,
In me confidit si quis, derisus abibit."

"I clothe the naked, despoil from those in garments clad,
If anyone in me confides, derided will he go from hence."

The portal below is borne on two columns resting on lions of red marble placed on each side of the door like couchant sentinels, and above is seen the divine hand held up in blessing with the words "Dextra Dei gentes benedicit sacra petentes" (God's right hand blesses those who sacred sites do haunt). On the portal are also scenes from the Bible and from the life of S. Zeno, the one in the centre being supposed to represent the deputation sent to him by the Emperor Gallienus. The doors are covered with panels of carved bronze reliefs (perhaps the oldest specimens of that form of metal decoration to be found in the country), and are said to belong to the ninth century. The scenes they represent are forty-eight in number, and are taken from the Old and New Testament. They are quaint and archaic to a degree, but the work is that of a bold and cunning craftsman, and the grotesque yet forcible attitudes of some of the personages (as, for example, Salome dancing before Herod) show the skill and humour that worked and lived in these men of old, hundreds of years ago. Within the doors a flight of steps leads down into the church, and one's impulse on entering is to stand at the head of those steps and gaze in silent admiration and reverence at the scene before one. It is so grand, so calm, so severe, so solid, and yet so graceful in the perfect proportion of lines, arches, columns, shafts. The nave extends between two side aisles in a line of faultless symmetry till it reaches in the centre to a double flight of stairs, the one flight leading down to the crypt, the upper and smaller one leading to the high altar and choir. To the right on entering is the baptismal font, formed from a single piece of marble, and designed by Brioletto, who was also the author of the window known as the Wheel of Fortune. On the other side is the famous "Coppa," or cup of S. Zeno, with the following legend attached to it: S. Zeno had freed a daughter of the Emperor Gallienus from an evil spirit which possessed her. The grateful father thereupon wished to present the saint with a crown of gold, but S. Zeno refused this and asked instead for a porphyry vase, which the demon, exorcised from the maiden, was ordered to carry from Rome to Verona. Crossing the Tiber the demon dropped the pedestal and arrived at Verona with the vase only. "Hie back," said S. Zeno, when the demon appeared with only half his burden, "and bring hither the other part as well." The order was obeyed, and that, too, in one moment of time, and only the crack in the vase bears witness to the small mishap which befel the precious cup in its transit from Rome to the place where it now stands.

S. ZENO MAGGIORE. CHOIR SCREEN AND ENTRANCE TO THE CRYPT

The columns in the nave are of different sizes and styles, and the capitals, most of them of pure Corinthian, are nearly all varied. The richness of originality and design shows to great advantage amidst the simplicity which exists on every side, and the freedom from an abundance of side-altars and—on the whole—from tawdriness of ornaments and paper flowers adds to the effect and dignity of the scene in a most grateful manner. A fine side-altar is to be noticed on the right going up the church, with four columns of reddish-brown marble all carved out of a single block, and resting on a lion and an ox, and dating from the fourteenth century. The walls are all of brick and of that picturesque stone known as "tufo" which we have had occasion to remark in nearly all the principal buildings in Verona. This "tufo" must be cut from the quarries in summer, when it hardens into such solidarity as to make it well-nigh everlasting. Should it be cut in winter its porous qualities remain and assert themselves, and it perishes and crumbles away in a short while. There can be little doubt that at one time the walls were all covered with frescoes, and even now many a one remains to testify to the piety and art that marked the twelfth, thirteenth and fourteenth centuries. Layard points this out in his valuable work so often referred to in these pages. He says:[63] "Like other Italian cities, Verona possessed, from a very early period, and before the revival of the arts in the thirteenth century, artists who decorated churches and public buildings with rude wall-paintings. Such early works are still to be seen in the ancient church of S. Zeno. They have no particular character or style to distinguish them from other productions of a similar kind." The balustrade that divides the nave from the choir and that stands above the arches over the crypt has on it a fine row of figures of our Lord and the twelve Apostles, a work that probably belongs to the end of the thirteenth century, or to even earlier days.

CHURCH OF S. ZENO, VERONA

The archways leading into the crypt are formed of perfect semicircles (of Roman as opposed to Byzantine shape) and contribute largely to the effect by which this low-lying and generally concealed portion of the church is brought into prominence. The pillars and columns in the crypt support a vaulted roof, through which some of them pierce into the choir above and carry on here the work begun on the lower floor. Some of these columns are very graceful, and would almost seem like feathers rising from the blocks of solid stone and masonry which are placed at limited intervals about the crypt. The capitals of these columns differ one from another; here and there they are quaint, not to say grotesque; others again are plain and classical, while one and all are in keeping with their surroundings, and bear witness to the love and skill that planned and placed them there. There are frescoes too upon the walls and about the columns, some very Byzantine in feeling and execution, some approaching again to the Giottesque period. Several saints and bishops are buried here—a solemn burial-place, and fitting for those who were the first to toil in the vineyard of souls at Verona, and whose earthly remains now rest from their labours in the beautiful crypt of S. Zeno. The sense of religion and devotion is enhanced by hanging lamps which cast an uncertain flickering light on the scene, and intensify the effect of shadow and shade that is thrown by the "shafts of shapely stone" clustering on every side. In the middle of the crypt stands the tomb of S. Zeno. The body lies in a bronze coffin, a fine piece of modern work by the brothers Spazzi (1889), guarded by seated figures of Faith, Hope, Charity and Religion. The whole is enclosed in the same kind of beautiful iron work such as has already been noticed round the tombs of the Scaligers, which was erected by order of Mastino II. della Scala.

Coming up from the crypt to the choir, the great picture by Andrea Mantegna hanging behind the high altar claims a careful study. The painting is on wood, in a lovely Renaissance frame which harmonises well with the decorative architectural detail in the picture. It was originally in six compartments, three above and three below, but was carried off to Paris by Napoleon, whence it was returned without the predella, which remained in the Salon carré of the Louvre (the present one at S. Zeno is a copy). The Blessed Virgin sits enthroned in the centre, holding the Child in the tender reverential manner to be found in the Bellini school, and supported by angels and cherubs. A lovely festoon of fruit and foliage is carried through the upper three compartments, caught up with red tassels, while the accessories of carpet, drapery, and hangings are extremely rich and glowing. St Peter, St Roch, St Paul, St John, and St Augustine are on the left of the picture; on the right are St John the Baptist, St Gregory, St Lawrence, and St Benedict; all the figures possessed of dignity and individuality, and expressing by their action or their attitude the characteristic peculiar to each one of them. "The Virgin is in a classic portico," says Mr Selwyn Brinton, "adorned with bas-reliefs, with festoons of fruit and coral. Eight robed child-angels of wonderful beauty play lutes, and sing beneath and beside her throne. She looks up, holding the beautiful Christ-child poised upright on her left hand; her expression and attitude seem full of quiet dignity. A masterpiece of his (Mantegna's) earlier style."[64]

The picture unfortunately is hung so high it is not easy to see, but a good view can be gained by clambering up the steps at the back of the altar where one is more on a level with it.

In the choir are some old carved walnut seats of the fourteenth century, and in an apse is a fresco of S. Zeno with his right hand raised in blessing. He is dressed in full episcopal robes, with a gorgeous dress of red, edged with gold, and lined with green, and with medallions of a particularly pretty shape studded about it. On the right hand of the choir is a quaint Giottesque fresco of St George, with his spear through the dragon's head, while the Princess stands by with a look which seems to imply that she would fain escape from knight and dragon alike did she but know how. St George's mantle flies in the breeze and reveals a beautiful lining of ermine; on his shield the Cross stands boldly out on a field of red, in harmonious keeping with the ermine-lined red cloak. The steed stands quietly by, and shows no apparent concern at the way in which his hind legs are encircled with coils of the dragon's body. Another fresco close by represents the raising of Lazarus, where most of the spectators hold their noses, remembering evidently Martha's caution as to the four days that her brother had spent beneath the sod! This fresco which is Byzantine in character is supposed to date from the eleventh century. Of the same, or maybe even an earlier date is a statue of S. Zeno, where his face is painted black (to remind us of his Eastern origin) and having a fish attached to his pastoral rod, a token of his profession as a fisher of souls.

Opening out from the church on the left hand side are the cloisters, of striking and original beauty. They were built in the twelfth century, and consist of twisted columns of red Verona marble, cut from a single block, and ingeniously held above and below by short pieces of marble. These were not added for the purpose but cut, together with the columns, out of the one solid bit of marble which served to form the whole. On the further side from the church the arches open out into a square form of arcading, the pillars here being larger than those of the actual cloisters. They were supposed to have stood round a sort of lavatory used probably by the monks either for themselves or for the vessels they required for their service.

CLOISTERS, S. ZENO MAGGIORE

Some fine tombs are placed here in the cloisters, resting on brackets on the wall, and belonging to the great families of Verona. There is a quaint saying as to some of these families that lie buried here, and that declares that they were: "Bevilacqua, che mai la bevero; Conti Verità, che mai la dissero; Conti Giusti che mai lo furono." (Bevilacqua—or Drink-water—who never drank it; Counts Verità—or Truth—who never said it; Counts Giusti—or Just—who never were it.) This saying certainly speaks better for the wit of the Veronese (which be it observed is known to be pithy and cutting) than for the manners of the gentry.

Here too is the tomb of Giuseppe, illegitimate son of Alberto della Scala, whom his father made Abbot of S. Zeno, and of whose appointment to that post notice has already been made.[65] Lana in his Commentary on the *Divina Commedia* speaking of the allusion made by Dante in the *Purgatorio*[66] to this transaction says: "Messer Alberto della Scala, who was aged had committed a great sin, in that he had made his son Abbot of S. Zeno, who was unworthy of such an episcopate; firstly, because he was infirm in the body; secondly, that he was defective in mind as in body; thirdly, that he was a natural son; so that he had these three great defects."[67]

Before leaving the church, and its pleasant well-informed custodian, one Lodovico Marchiori, whose family have carried on that office for one hundred and eighty-seven years, some attention must be given to the campanile of S. Zeno, which is one of the finest in Verona, if not in Italy. It was begun in 1045, and finished in 1178, and is a grand square tower surmounted with a spire which has four corner turrets set on a double row of arches. A quaint Latin inscription on the north side of the belfry, and dating from the beginning of the fifteenth century tells how there rests here one Henry of Tearen,[68] whose only claim to celebrity seems to have been that he was the husband of Gertrude! Who Gertrude was does not transpire, but the evidence that even in those days a man could be no more than the husband of his wife would seem to imply that the "new woman" was not so much a creation of these days as a continuation of a state of things recognised centuries ago and worthy to be recorded for all time.

To the left side of the façade of S. Zeno rises a square brick tower with forked battlements. This is all that remains of the actual monastery that belonged to the church, and within whose walls kings and emperors had found hospitality when in days of old they sojourned for a while in the fair city of Verona la Degna.

CHAPTER XIII

Verona and its Crown of Castles

THERE is another side of Verona to be studied apart from that connected with her glorious churches and other buildings. To wander through the squares and streets, studying the battlements and towers, and noting the outdoor existence, so to speak, of the town is necessary to a thorough understanding and enjoyment of the place. In this way we shall realise the balconies which form so beautiful and special a feature in the picturesque loveliness of the town, and of which Ruskin speaks as follows: "The chief city of Italy, as regards the strict effect of the balcony, is Verona; and if we were once to lose ourselves among the sweet shadows of its lonely streets, where the falling branches of the flowers stream like fountains through the pierced traceries of the marble, there is no saying whether we might be able to return to our immediate work."[69]

Nor must the doorways be overlooked, those grand old arches of red Verona marble—generally of Renaissance style—denoting the entrance to many a noble palace, and often, alas! being the only trace now left of some once princely residence. The acquaintance thus gained of the exterior of the town will lead us on maybe to more outlying places, and tempt us to make expeditions to some of the old castles which stand around Verona. Of these castles mention will only be made of those which still boast of standing walls, or of ruins which are sufficiently imposing to be worth a visit, and whose beauty or historic merit will reward the trouble taken to reach them. Four of such castles, Montorio, Illasi, Tregnano, Soave, stand on the left bank of the Adige; on the right bank the castles—five in number—are Villafranca, Valeggio, Nogarole, Sanguinetto, Sirmione.

There is little to be said about some of these castles from an historic point of view. Their origin is lost in the remote past; and in cases such as those of Montorio and Tregnano it can only be said that they formed strong fortresses in the line of defence above Verona, and were additional gems in the crown poised above the city, and which contributed at once to her beauty and security. Montorio would certainly seem to have dated from the time of the Romans, were it only for the amount of coins and inscriptions belonging to that period which have been found there. Tregnano, lying in the valley of Illasi, is of an older date, according to Cipolla, than Soave, though of smaller proportions. The chief point of interest yet remaining is a grand old pentagonal tower. From this a wall branches out which surrounds the castle and which has small towers at intervals, all of a most simple form. More than one fine castle stands in this same valley of Illasi, but the best known is the one which takes its name from the valley. It was presented to the Scaligers by Pope Nicholas III., and, with the other possessions of the della Scalas, shared the same fate that made the lords of Milan, and of Padua, and the Venetian Republic, owners in turn of their goods and wealth. In the sixteenth century Illasi passed into the hands of the Veronese patricians, the Counts Pompei; and their villas and houses form one of the chief features of the site, situated as they are at the foot of the hill on which is perched the castle, and from where Ruskin wrote the beautiful description of the view obtained from here, and which is given in chapter x., p. 229.

RUINS OF THE VILLA OF CATULLO

In 1885 Count Antonio Pompei, the last direct descendant of this great family, died. These Counts of Illasi, who had received their title from the Venetian Republic early in the sixteenth century (with the obligation of offering every year a wax taper of the value of a ducat to the Church of St Mark in Venice), received many and lasting honours from other states and sovereigns. The Emperor Charles V.

conferred the rights of citizens of Milan on them; the same privilege with regard to the town of Mantua was granted by Duke Ferdinand Charles; and Henry IV. allowed them to quarter the lilies of France on their shield. This last Count of Illasi (whose family is now merged in that of the Counts Perez) was a worthy descendant of a long line of jurisconsults, lawyers, writers, poets, ambassadors, generals and knights. He was himself an archæologist, and a writer too on such matters. He had been present in his youth at the demolition of an old wall of the Castle of Illasi, and on that occasion came across a sad and undoubted evidence of a tragedy that had occurred in his family many hundreds of years previously. The skeleton of a woman was found in this wall, heavily laden with chains, and the story goes that it was certainly that of the Countess Ginevra, the wife of Count Girolamo Pompei, whose infidelity to her husband had been avenged in this awful way. No hope of escape for the wife whom he knew false! No mercy for her who had proved unfaithful! Only the chains weighing heavily on her young and lovely limbs; the wall slowly closing in upon her; the lingering death of agony and starvation; the remorse when alone she faced her doom;—can a fate more terrible be imagined? or a vengeance more complete have been exacted?

The last castle on the left bank of the Adige, that of Soave, is without doubt the most interesting of all these strongholds, and should certainly not be left unvisited. The tramway which starts just outside the Porta Vescovo takes one there in a good hour. The journey lies through a flat country, fertile with corn, maize, and vines, and leading up to the hills which rise "on and always on" till they are lost in the distant horizon. A short walk under an avenue of "Paulownia Imperialis" leads to the old town, which is girt with a circuit of brick battlemented walls, perfect both as to condition and construction. A grand double archway, on which is carved the arms of the Scaligers, opens into the town, while at its further end is a stone pathway which leads up a steep incline to the castle perched on the top. The position is splendid, overlooking miles of plain, and bounded on the northern side by the heights of Monte Lessini. The building takes us back in fancy to some of our old Norman fortresses, for here too is the moat, the drawbridge, the portcullis, and all that goes to form a feudal stronghold. The moat though is now dried up and overgrown with vegetation, and the walls are of brick as opposed to stone, albeit of such beautiful masonry as to arouse no sense of disparaging comparison. Crossing the drawbridge under a grand archway with the portcullis set in the brickwork, we gain the first courtyard, which opens again through another doorway into a second and inner courtyard. The banqueting hall probably stood here of old, or it may be the kitchen, to judge from the outline of a huge chimney which can yet be traced clearly and which evidently once towered high up into the air. From here, stooping low under a small archway, we come into an enclosed square, not large as to circumference, but shut in to the extent of some sixty feet in height. Prisoners or criminals were thrown down into this hold, and those who did not die of the shock or fall (and they would be the exceptions) were left to linger till death released them from their sufferings. A fine old well stands in the last and inner courtyard, its edges worn away inside with the marks of the ropes which for centuries have performed their office of drawing water—and very good water too—from the old well. On the ground floor of this portion of the castle is a vaulted chamber said to have been the guard-room, and from there a narrow staircase leads up to the only part of the building that would be habitable did its owner choose to live in it. The rooms, consisting of a bedroom, sitting-room and dining-room, are kept though more for show than for use; and from the dining-room one passes through a small anteroom up a narrow stone staircase on to the battlements. An excellent view is had from here of the castle itself, its turrets, inner courts, grass slopes, and steep parapets, to the little town sheltering in true feudal fashion at the foot of the castle. The city walls are also clearly discernible from this height, forming as they do an uninterrupted square of turreted walls, each turret or tower equidistant from its neighbour, and presenting as perfect an example of a mediæval stronghold as can well be seen anywhere. The good woman who acts as "custode" has a ready story of how the Scaligers who built and owned this fortress existed long before the birth of Christ, and had indeed inhabited it in those far-off ages. The real tale is that the name of Soave came from a colony of Swabians (Svevi or Suabi) who came into Italy, with Otho I. of Germany, and settled there. It is also very probable that the Romans had once built on those heights and laid the foundations of the citadel which the Scaligers perfected in after times. Such an hypothesis gains ground from the number of Roman coins, pins, fibulæ, inscriptions, stones, and so forth that have been found in and around Soave, and that are all collected and kept in the old castle. Its present state of preservation is owing to the Senator Camuzzoni, whose one thought and care has been to restore the castle on its original lines and guard it intact from injury or decay.

Soave is also celebrated for an excellent white wine which hails from there; by no means feeble as to character, and as famous in its way as its red neighbour from the Val Policella. Another white wine, also very good, is made at Soave, called Vino Santo. This however is sweet, and commends itself more as a liqueur than as a beverage. The little town too is full of interest, and many an hour might be whiled away in this mediæval hamlet did the castles lying on the right bank of the Adige not claim a passing notice in their turn.

CASTLE OF SIRMIONE

The first of these in geographical order is the castle of Villafranca Veronese, so called to distinguish it from the other seven and twenty Villafrancas which are said to lie scattered over the face of the globe. It lies between Verona and Mantua, and owes its fame in modern days to the peace signed here, 12th July 1859, between the Emperors of Austria and France, when Lombardy was ceded to Italy, and a very forward step taken in the events which culminated in Italian unity and independence. The cause that led originally to the erection of the fortress was as follows:—The Veronese had built a castle at Ostiglia on the Po, a castle that was of all-important moment to them from a military and commercial point of view. The frequent inundations of the river had damaged the fort, and the Veronese saw fit to repair it. The inhabitants of Mantua were annoyed that this frontier town should be put into a condition to resist their incursions, and they determined to molest the works, or if possible to prevent them altogether. This resolution annoyed the Veronese not a little. The Mantuans however persisted, and finally both parties resorted to arms. The Veronese were victors in the fight; but the Mantuans only prepared for further action, and resolved on being revenged. To guard against any surprises the Veronese set to work to erect a fort in an advanced and advantageous spot, and chose Villafranca for the purpose. The works were at once begun; in 1202 the castle was finished, and a good body of soldiers were placed in it to guard against any attack or invasion from the south. The walls and bastions are of remarkable solidity and thickness, and the fortress of Villafranca may certainly rank as one of the strongest and most imposing to be seen in Italy. The sole object of its erection was for defence, and it has fulfilled its purpose absolutely. Scenes of violence, of siege, and of fire have occurred within its walls, but no tales of love or romance, which for the most part lighten the story of many a gloomy massive pile, are forthcoming from the sombre stronghold of Villafranca. It was closely besieged in 1233 by Ezzelino da Romano, when several Guelph leaders from Verona and the neighbourhood defended it.

The Story of Verona

The people of Mantua at that epoch supported the Guelph faction and took the part of Riccardo da Sambonifacio against the Ghibellines. To strengthen themselves against these incursions of the Mantuans, the people of Verona aided their Podestà Enrico d'Egna to add to the fortress of Villafranca, and a massive tower (such as is to be seen in well-nigh every mediæval fortress of importance) was built, together with a moat. The love of building possessed to such a remarkable degree by the Scaligers was brought into play by them at Villafranca; and Mastino II. wishing to protect himself still further against Mantua, began the erection of the great wall known as the "Serraglio," and leading from Villafranca towards the enemy's territory. The outbreak of a pestilence in Verona in 1349 (the very year in which the "Serraglio" was begun) stopped the work, which was finished under Cangrande II., the son and successor of Mastino II. This stupendous work, consisting of towers at stated intervals with ditches and moats behind which to shelter the peasants with their flocks and herds, brought Villafranca almost into touch with Valeggio (another castle soon to be mentioned) and acted as a mighty rampart between the territory belonging to Verona, and that owned by the lords of Mantua.

In 1404 the inhabitants of Mantua took refuge within the fortress of Villafranca to protect themselves against the forces of Galeazzo Gonzaga, who was determined to become lord of Mantua, and whose rule met with bitter opposition. The men of Mantua set fire to their houses and fled with their wives and children and chattels to the rock of Villafranca. Gonzaga irritated at this opposition resolved to quell it and assaulted the fort with violence. In vain he tried every artifice that strength and ingenuity could suggest. His forces were driven back at every point. He lost heavily, and retired at length after three days of uninterrupted attack to Vigasio, resolved to return with renewed forces and take vengeance on the bold defenders of their homes and hearths. Other sieges took place at Villafranca often and again in the course of the fifteenth century, but neither then nor in later times were its strongholds or towers destroyed by foe or fire, and it stands to this day a marvel of strength and resistance, its sternness softened by the nursery gardens kept within its courtyards where the grace and beauty of vegetable life contrast in soft and gentle harmony with the solidity and masonic craft of bygone ages.

At a distance of five miles from Villafranca is the castle of Valeggio on the banks of the Mincio. It was either built or rebuilt by Cangrande II. della Scala, and may very probably have been set up by that prince as the complement to the great wall of the "Serraglio" which was finished during his reign. It boasts a number of subterranean passages, vaults, and dungeons, and together with Borghetto, which stands on the opposite height, occupies an important military position, commanding the passage of the Mincio. The view from the castle terrace is not only grand, but full of interest and association for every lover of Italian history and of Italian independence. On one side is to be seen a stately old square tower, which stands above the memorable field of Solferino. On another side is the Tower of San Martino, and again to the West rises high in the distance the column that marks where the bones of the dead were laid to rest after the "day of pride and sorrow" of Custozza. Valeggio is celebrated too for the marvellous stone bridge constructed by Gian Galeazzo Visconti, duke of Milan at the close of the fourteenth century to strengthen himself against Francesco Gonzaga, lord of Mantua. To relate all the intrigues and quarrels which led to the erection of this bridge over the Mincio would be out of place here; suffice it to say that it was laid on a Roman substructure, and had high gateways with towers at each end, while the arches of the bridge spanned the river. Only one arch remains now, but the ruin shows what a colossal work it was, worthy even in its decay of the titles of "famous," "gigantic," "most noble," and "magnificent" that have been lavished on it by different writers. The ulterior purpose of the bridge is yet a matter of discussion, and historians are still at variance as to whether Gian Galeazzo built the bridge with the intent to alter the course of the river, or to raise for himself a causeway into the Veronese territory.

History and tradition have alike little to say about Nogarole, beyond the fact that it was built by Mastino II. della Scala against the Mantuans. The old castle, situated at no great distance from Villafranca, no doubt derived its name at some time or other from the family of Nogarola, a family which figured so often and so honourably in the story of Verona, and of whom the last remaining member died only a few years ago.

Sanguinetto is one of the few castles under discussion that has no associations with the great house of the Scaligers beyond the fact that Bartolomeo and Antonio della Scala gave over the castle in 1376 to their general Jacopo del Verme. It has, in common with all the villages and towns in the province of Verona, many and evident traces of Roman life and habits. The castle was the scene of much fighting in the Middle Ages, and that it was used also as prison is clearly proved by the discovery made there some fifty years ago of a skeleton in armour which was found enclosed in the walls. The grand old castle was sadly damaged in 1800, and what has escaped the ravages of time and the destroying hand of man is now preserved with care by the municipality, and used for public offices.

It only remains now to speak of Sirmione, the most interesting perhaps after Soave, of the sites around Verona, and which the traveller should on no account omit to visit. The Peninsula of Sirmione on the Lake of Garda was famed

The Story of Verona

in Roman times, and is a spot whose praises have been sung by bards in all ages and tongues. Covered with olive and bay trees it would seem to invite poets to inhabit its groves, and to chant of the soft balmy air that floats round its shores. Hills and gentle slopes alternate with the level swards on which villages and villas are dotted at intervals, bringing life and movement to the scene and imparting a spirit of animation to this otherwise secluded spot. In the days of the Romans it was prosperous and active. They surrounded it with walls and entered it on their maps as a strategical point, possessing besides a secure camp and a strong station. There were also many luxurious villas here inhabited by nobles of wealth and position, among them being the one owned by Catullus's father, a man whose fortune allowed of his entertaining Julius Cæsar, and whose habitation at the northern extremity of the peninsula must have been splendid judging from the ruins which are pointed out to this day as those of the Grotto of Catullus.

One of the chief objects that catches the eye on alighting at the southern end is the castle of the Scaligers. Their heraldic badge of the ladder (scala) is on the door, and the manifestation of their might and power is alike visible in the great wall which surrounds the castle, and which fortifies it on the side sloping down to the lake as well as on the land side. A moat runs below this outer wall, and in front of the chief entrance are evidences of a drawbridge which must once have stood there. The entrance has two approaches, one by which carriages and wheeled vehicles could pass, the other for foot passengers. The actual plan of the castle is a quadrangle, but there are inner walls and courtyards of different heights and elevations, and towers at stated distances break up the effect of evenness presented to the eye, and result in a picturesque and formidable-looking citadel. The castle had three entrances, two by land, and one on to the lake, both those by land being approached by drawbridges. The interior of the castle was formed of two divisions, and the masonry of these courts is as perfect as it can be, and fit to be compared with the finest and best Roman work.

"Out upon Time! who for ever will leave
But enough of the Past for the Future to grieve!"

These walls are now in ruin; decay is over a building which would seem to have once defied even Time itself; the owl and the bat haunt the chambers that rang with mirth and joyaunce when "high dames and mighty earls" held court there, and when the chase and the dance followed each other in quick succession, and all seemed made for merriment and happiness.

There was prosperity for the inhabitants of the land in the Scaligers' time, but there was sorrow and mourning too, for the lords of Verona were not always mild rulers, and any opposition to their ideas or wishes was apt to meet with a severity of the harshest kind. Such was the case when the sect known as the Patarins (Patarini, or Catari) set up their religious tenets against those of their liege lords. These tenets (which the historians of Sirmione confess frankly have never met with an exponent who has clearly revealed them) appear to have resembled in some way the doctrines of the Manichæans. They were persecuted, outlawed, and burnt by popes, emperors, and kings. Their courage, or (as their enemies called it) their audacity, made them assert themselves again and again, and, when possible, turn the arm of persecution on their persecutors. They had however need of some spot where they could be safe from their foes, and Sirmione seemed to them a haven where they could retire and pursue their worship unmolested. They reckoned without their host. Mastino I. della Scala, then lord of Verona, and consequently of Sirmione as well, was made aware of the heresy which infected his lands, and which was spreading rapidly round his castle. A commission was formed to inquire into the evil, and to extirpate it if possible. Remonstrance however failed to do much, though a few acknowledged the error of their ways, and were received afresh into the true fold with many injunctions and admonitions, all, we are told, of a most benign and fatherly nature. We can hardly say as much for the punishment meted out to the obdurate.

They were condemned to be burnt to death, and no less than a hundred (some say 150, and some 75) men and women were brought to Verona and there suffered at the stake in the Arena (1276). Mastino's zeal met with a handsome recompense, for the Pope, Nicholas III., bestowed on him the castle of Illasi with its feudal rights and privileges.

It is not stated definitely if Dante visited Sirmione, but his knowledge of the country around, of the Benaco, and so forth, may be taken as evidence that he had been there, and spoke of these places from his personal knowledge of them.

Sirmione followed the fortunes of Verona. After the fall of the Scaligers (all of whom were liberal and generous patrons of the place), it became subject to the Visconti, then to the Carraresi, and finally it came under the rule of the Venetian Republic.

Its condition for many years was that of extreme poverty and misery. A few fishermen carried on a hard and unprofitable trade; no travellers halted at a spot that boasted only bad accommodation; and the outlook for a while was deplorable. All that however is now changed. The discovery of some hot sulphur springs has brought doctors and strangers in abundance to the place. Baths and hotels are already set up, and though the quiet, picturesque past is threatened with an overflow of modern buildings, fashions, and elegance (so-called), let us hope that the inhabitants at all events will profit by these innovations, even if the artist and archæologist may sigh over them.

CHAPTER XIV

Plan for seeing the Town—Hotels

THE length of a traveller's sojourn in Verona is generally a short one, and the outside of his visit is at the most from three to four days. The time is short for seeing and understanding the town, and the following plan is sketched out so as to include the principal sights and to lay before the passer-by as good an idea as can be had in a limited time of the chief centres of interest in Verona:—

(1)	The Church of Sant' Anastasia, beside which stands the famous tomb of Guglielmo da Castelbarco (p. 160, etc.); along the Via Liceo and down the Via Duomo to the Duomo; S. Giovanni in Fonte; the Vescovado, and by by-ways to the Piazza delle Erbe (which can never be seen too often) into the Piazza dei Signori, or Piazza Dante, to the tombs of the Scaligers and the little Church of Sta. Maria Antica (chapters vii. and viii.).
(2)	Through the Piazza delle Erbe, down the Via Cappello and the Via S. Sebastiano, etc., to the Church of S. Fermo. Then across the Adige by the Ponte delle Navi to the Museo Civico, or Picture Gallery (chapter ix.).

(3)	By the Corso Cavour (see St Eufemia, Porta dei Borsari, and Castel Vecchio on the way—chapter xi.) to the Church of S. Zeno (chapter xii.), and from there to S. Bernardino, driving round through the Porta Palio and Porta Nuova to the Arena (chapter ii.).
(4)	Across the Ponte di Pietra to the chief churches on the other side of the Adige, S. Giorgio in Braida; S. Stefano, Sta. Maria in Organo; and, if time allows of it, a visit to the Giardino Giusti (chapter x.).

A delightful expedition, occupying a good four hours, can be had by tram or carriage, to Soave, but a little walking is required to go right up to the Castle of the Scaligers, perched above the old walled-in town (chapter xiii.).

The best hotel in Verona is the Hôtel de Londres, also known as that of the Deux Tours. Part of the building is said to have once formed part of the Palace of the Scaligers, a statement that may well be the case, given its position and proximity to the house once inhabited by the lords of Verona. Here too is a good guide, one Illuminato Veronesi, who speaks English and knows his Verona well.

The Hôtel S. Lorenzo is pleasantly placed near the banks of the Adige. The Hôtel Colomba d'Oro stands in the Via Colomba, and is not far from the Piazza Vittorio Emanuele and the Arena.

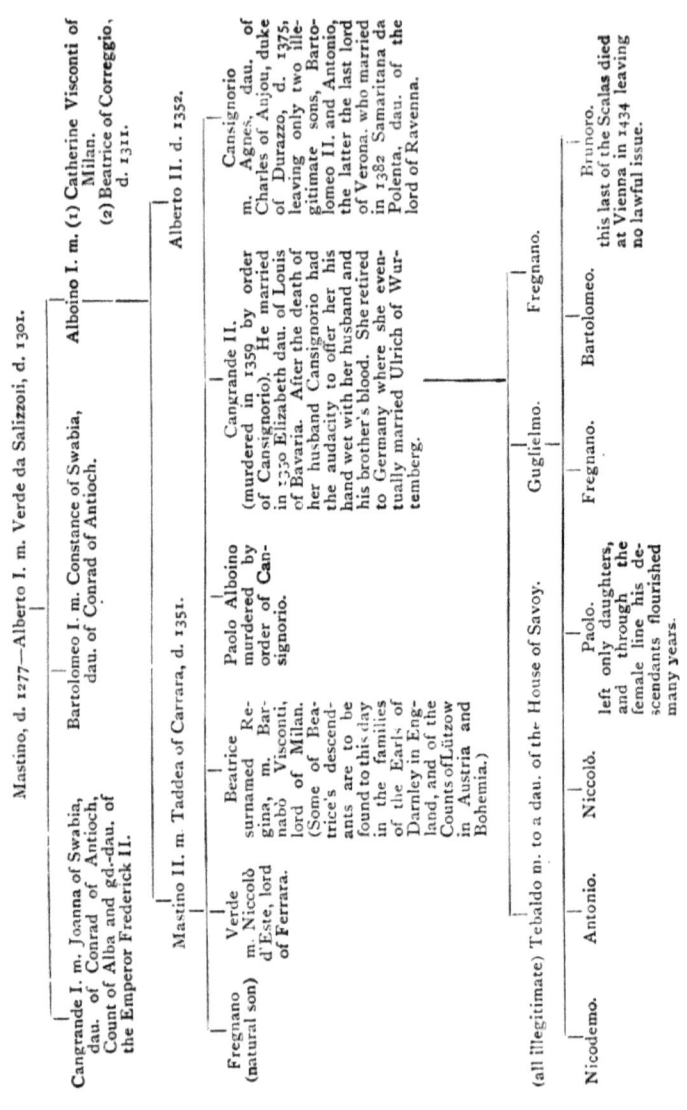

VERONA
GENEALOGICAL TABLE OF THE SCALIGERS.

*FROM AN ENGRAVING OF THE YEAR 1535 IN THE
BIBLIOTECA COMUNALE OF VERONA SHOWING
THE OLD WALLS ROUND THE TOWN*

VERONA

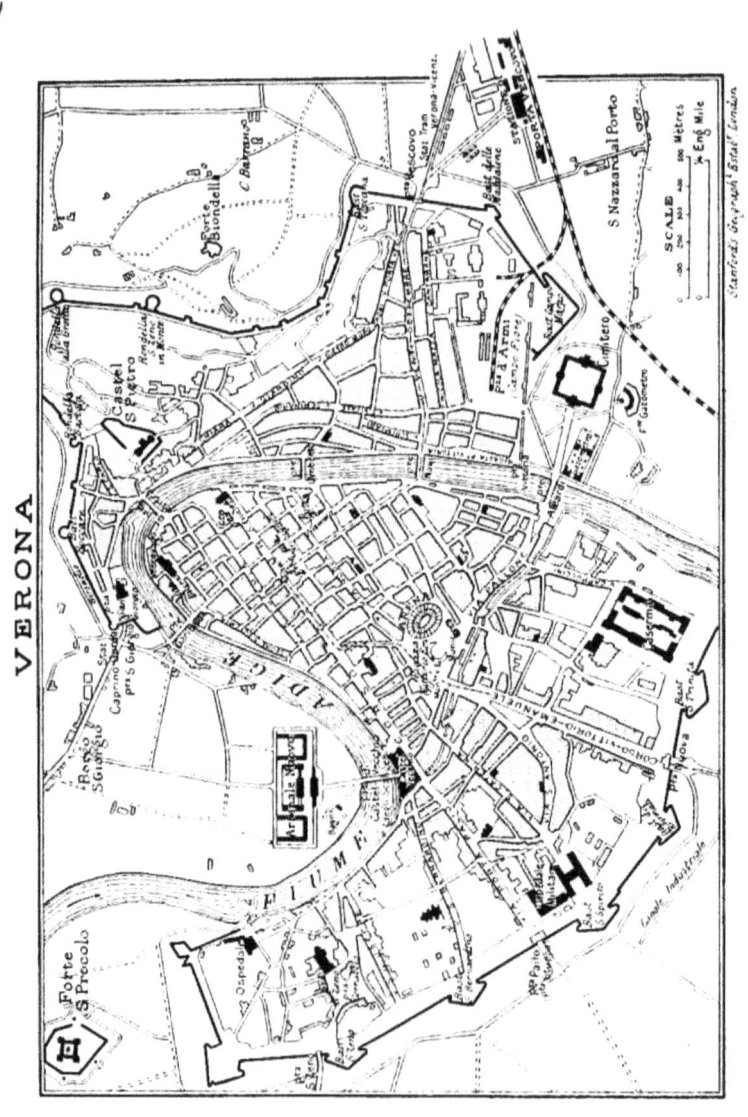

FOOTNOTES:

[1] Ruskin, Verona and other Lectures. Allen (1894).

[2] Gibbon, The History of the Decline and Fall of the Roman Empire. London, Murray, 1887, vol. ii., ch. xiv., p. 129.

[3] See chapter x.

[4] Benvenuti de Rambaldis de Imola, Comentum Super Dantis Aldighierij Comoediam. Tr. by the Hon. William Warren Vernon: Readings on the Purgatorio. London, Macmillan, 1897.

[5] "In an amphitheatre, 'podium' was the name for a railed basement which ran like a high enclosure round the whole circumference of the arena." See Mollett, J. W., An illustrated Dictionary of Words used in Art and Archæology. London, Sampson Low, 1883.

[6] The extravagance in which Samaritana indulged contributed in no small degree to the decline and fall of her husband's house. Her taste for jewellery was of a most ridiculous—not to say vulgar order. She heaped on jewels in profusion and would not put on her stockings unless they

too were decorated with precious stones! She also excited the indignation of contemporary chroniclers by her insistance in sending to Ostiglia for some special unguents which she deemed necessary for beautifying her hair, and which were conveyed to this port on the Po at great expense from distant towns.

[7] Zagata.

[8] Belviglieri, Verona e Provincia, p. 341.

[9] It may be well to remind the reader that this arch which was taken down in 1805 stood originally near Castel Vecchio, and was the work of the famous architect Vitruvius Cerdone, whose name was engraved on the archway. The inscriptions formerly existing over the niches show that the statues belonging to them were of the Gavii family. Panvinio is of opinion that the arch was erected to the memory of that Gavius who was consul B.C. 145. Maffei on the other hand says that it was set up to the memory of the whole of the Gavii family.

[10] C. Cipolla, Compendio della Storia Politica di Verona. Verona, 1899.

[11] Histoire des Républiques Italiennes, Sismonde de Sismondi, Bruxelles, 1838, vol. i., ch. xv., p. 507.

[12] Alexander IV. issued letters for this crusade in 1255. It was preached next year by the Archbishop of Ravenna.

[13] J. A. Symonds, Age of the Despots. London, Smith, Elder & Co., 1898, ch. iii., p. 83, &c.

[14]
"Tenne ambo le chiavi
Del cuor di Federigo."—Inf. xiii. 58-59.

[15] "Tiranni Che diér nel Sangue e nell' aver di piglio."—Inf. xii. 104-105

[16] I am aware that I am destroying a legend that has found its way into nearly every guide-book and even into some histories of Verona by this assertion. But no Veronese of any culture or learning supports the popular tradition, or admits that the deed aroused such horror in the public mind as to brand the spot with a special name. The "Volto Barbaro" simply took its name from the Barbaro family who lived there, as the "Volto Marioni" in another part of the town did from the Marioni family—a fact that no one versed in Veronese matters would ever seek to gainsay or dispute.

[17] Giuseppe Biadego, Dante e gli Scaligeri, Venezia, 1899.

[18] See Cipolla, op. cit. p. 208.

[19]
"Thine earliest refuge and thine earliest inn
Shall be the mighty Lombard's courtesy,
Who on the ladder bears the holy bird,
Who such benign regard shall have for thee
That 'twixt you twain, in doing and in asking,
That shall be first which is with others last.
With him shalt thou see one who at his birth
Has by this star of strength been so impressed,
That notable shall his achievements be."
Paradiso, canto xvii., 76, &c.
(Longfellow's Translation).

[20] Giuseppe Biadego, op. cit., p. 12.

[21] Op. cit., p. 13.

[22] Boccaccio, Giornata I., Novella VII.

[23] Gio. Villani, Istorie fiorentine, lib. x., cap. 139.

[24] I have taken this translation from the Notes on the Paradiso, given in Longfellow's translation of the Divine Comedy (London, 1877). From there, too, have I taken the extract from Petrarch, which is to be found in Balbo's Life of Dante, translated by Mrs Bunbury, ii. 207.

[25]
Ch'io veggio certamente, e per☒ il narro,
A darne tempo, gia stelle propinque,
Sicure d'ogni intoppo e d'ogni sbarro;
Nel quale un cinquecento diece e cinque,
Messo di Dio, ancideră la fuja
Conquel gigante che con lei delinque.

[26] Vernon, Hon. William Warren, Readings on the Purgatorio of Dante. London, Macmillan, 1889, vol. ii., p. 429, &c.

[27] Rithmi de obitu Henrici VII., ed. Freher, Germanie-rerum Scriptores, i. 15, etc.

[28] Cipolla, C, Storia delle Signorie italiani dal 1313 al 1350. Milano, 1881, lib. i. iv.

[29] I have not gone into the lengthy and vexed question of the date of Cangrande's birth. The year generally accepted is 1291, and that I have followed as the most probable one, and the one most deserving of acceptance.

[30] Cipolla, op. cit. lib. i. iv.

[31] Verona and other Lectures. Allen, Orpington, 1894.

[32] This is not the place to enlarge on the fine character and qualities of Regina della Scala; but it is interesting to note that one of the most famous theatres in Italy takes its name from her, and that the "Scala" at Milan was so called in honour of this daughter of Verona.

[33] Op. cit. p. 17.

[34] See pp. 30-31.

[35] P. Sgulmero.

[36] Published anonymously in 1799 by Cristoforo Tentori.

[37] Selwyn Brinton, The Renaissance in Italian Art, Part II., p. 37. Simpkin, London, 1898.

[38] Op. cit. p. 38, etc.

[39] Op. cit. p. 42.

[40] Handbook of Painting. The Italian schools—based on the handbook of Kugler—thoroughly revised and in part rewritten by Sir A. Henry Layard, London. Murray, 1887. Part I. p. 274.

[41] The Stones of Venice. John Ruskin, London. Smith, Elder & Co., 1858. Vol. i., Appendix 8, p. 361.

[42]
The artificer Nicholas who carved these things,
The folk who here collect will praise for aye.

[43] Op. cit. p. 59.

[44] Since the above was written it has now (April 1902) been replaced above the chapel; but so high up as to be seen with difficulty.

[45] Ruskin, Stories of Venice, vol. i. Appendix 19.

[46] In this courtyard much might be done were the Town Council of Verona only as ready to lay out sums in guarding and preserving their old treasures as they are in erecting modern houses and "embellishments" to attract visitors to their city. Some fine arches dating from the time of the Scaligers remain here blocked up; and some lovely frescoes which ask only to be protected from sun and rain cry aloud in this Cortile for an attention which is persistently denied them.

[47] Ruskin, Stones of Venice, op. cit. vol. iii. p. 70, etc.

[48] The tablet runs as follows:—
Queste furono le case
Dei Capuleti
Onde uscì la Giulietta
Per cui
Tanto piansero i cuori gentili
E i poeti cantarono.
These were the houses
Of the Capulets
From whence sprang Juliet
For whom
So many gentle hearts have wept

And poets have sung.

[49] Op. cit. Part 1. p. 268.

[50] Op. cit. p. 59.

[51] Op. cit. p. 64.

[52] Op. cit. Part I. p. 264.

[53] Ruskin, Verona and other Lectures. Allen, 1894.

[54] Op. cit. p. 264.

[55] Selwyn Brinton, op. cit. p. 58, etc.

[56] Spaventi-Guida di Verona, p. 132.

[57] The authorship of this picture is open to doubt. It has been attributed to different masters in turn. Mr Berenson is of opinion that it is by Girolamo Mocetto, an opinion also held by Crowe and Cavalcaselle.

[58] C. Cipolla, Compendio della Storia Politica di Verona. Verona 1899. pp. 46 and 44.

[59] Layard, op. cit. p. 268.

[60] Layard, op. cit. p. 263.

[61]
... "and seemed to be of those
Who at Verona run for the green mantle
Across the plain; and seemed to be among them
The one who wins, and not the one who loses."
—(Longfellow's Translation.)

[62] Readings on the Inferno of Dante, Hon. William Warren Vernon (London: Macmillan, 1894), vol. i. p. 532, etc.

[63] Layard, op. cit. Part I. p. 253.

[64] Selwyn Brinton, op. cit. p. 53.

[65] In chapter vi.

[66] Purgatorio, xviii. 124.

[67] La Divina Commedia, col commento di Jacopo della Lana, Bologna, 1866, 3 vols. 8vo.

[68] Hic reqviescit Heinricus de Tearen se maritus Gertrvdis.

[69] Ruskin, op. cit. vol. ii. ch. vii. p. 248.

www.ingramcontent.com/pod-product-compliance
Lightning Source LLC
Chambersburg PA
CBHW021143160426
43194CB00007B/670